TO LIVE LONG ENOUGH

NAUM JASNY
Courtesy of *U. S. News & World Report*

TO LIVE LONG ENOUGH

The Memoirs of
Naum Jasny, Scientific Analyst

Edited, with Biographical Commentaries

by

Betty A. Laird

and

Roy D. Laird

THE UNIVERSITY PRESS OF KANSAS
Lawrence—Manhattan—Wichita

Library of Congress Cataloging in Publication Data
Jasny, Naum, 1883-1967.
　　To live long enough.

　　Includes bibliographical references and index.
　　"Publications by Naum Jasny": p.
　　1. Jasny, Naum, 1883-1967. 2. Economists—Corre-
spondence, reminiscences, etc. 3. Agriculturists—Cor-
respondence, reminiscences, etc. I. Laird, Betty A.
II. Laird, Roy D. III. Title.
HB113.J3A35　　1976　　330.9'2'4　　75-33900
ISBN 0-7006-0140-6

Preface

Naum Mikhailovich Jasny (1883-1967) was born a citizen of the
tsarist empire, the son of an extremely successful and wealthy Jewish
businessman. Russia, Austria (briefly), Germany, and finally the
United States were his homes. As a young man in search of himself,
he studied in several European and Russian universities. His many
careers included that of a lawyer (without paying clients), a successful businessman, a revolutionary (Menshevik in persuasion), a political refugee, a bureaucrat (both for the 1917 Provisional Government
and later, while in Germany, for the Soviets), a teacher, and a highly
productive research scholar. Although he felt that he had not found
his place until well into his thirties, the balance of his life and all of
his passion came to be dedicated to the pursuit of truth.

From the beginning of his career as a researcher in Russia
(where his findings were contrary to his family's milling interests),
there was no conflict of interest that blocked his search for understanding. Starting in Russia, he very frequently was in the center of
major controversy (sometimes bitter) with colleagues and associates.
Editors, particularly, were necessary evils who tried to change words
and thus spoiled the nuances of meaning. Yet, all respected his enormous contributions. Rarely were the arguments over personalities;
mostly they centered on substantive issues; for he was a research
giant, one of the great pioneers in interpreting Soviet affairs.

As it must always have been, a visit to Jasny's Washington, D.C.,
apartment in his later years was a most rewarding experience for a
young colleague, come to sit at the feet of the master. Movement

about the rooms was a difficult maneuver among his research materials. Piled high on the tables and chairs and in the corners were books, journals, and papers. "What was Khrushchev up to in his campaign to plow up millions of acres of virgin and arid lands?" Unerringly, a copy of *Pravda* was extracted from a pile on the table, an issue several months old of *Voprosy ekonomiki* (Problems of Economics) was taken from a stack in the corner, and pieces of the puzzle that fit together began to emerge. After a while, a bottle of light wine was taken from the refrigerator (where also was the stock of candy for the neighborhood children who were the sparkle of his life), but the discussion, probing, and exchange of ideas and findings never flagged, ending only when the exhausted student excused himself from the most exacting of seminars.

Although he produced hundreds of articles and over twenty books and monographs, his 837-page study *The Socialized Agriculture of the USSR* alone is a monumental achievement, unmatched by most productive scholars in a lifetime of work. With only his pencil he made the calculations and produced the text and numerous detailed tables and graphs, which at first were severely challenged by some, but almost all of which eventually proved to be correct. No wonder one of his passions came to be baseball, particularly the intricacies of its statistical records.

To know the life and work of Naum Jasny is to understand better both the revolution that occurred in Russia in 1917 and the successes and failures of the Soviet system that followed. Even more, however, his work was a supreme example of what must be done if the bits and pieces of data are to be torn from that bitch-goddess who jealously guards the vault of truth. For those who think of scholarship as a narrow pursuit (blinders in place) of odd facts, Jasny does not fit the picture. For those who see the pursuit of new understanding as a dedication to follow wherever the precarious paths may lead, he was a scholar's researcher, whether he was interpreting Soviet industrial policy or exploring the mystery of grains in antiquity.

He was a young revolutionary in the 1905–1917 era, but his dedication to fact (surely more than his personality as such, as he suggested) got in the way of his contribution to the fighting. However disenchanted he had become with the tsarist establishment, the interests that fired his imagination and stimulated his efforts were on the constructive side. Thus, even though in later years he expressed doubt as to the value of his work in 1917, his major contribution at the time was to provide the Provisional Government with the base for some of its first, most crucial legislation—a scheme to maximize the availability of food in the face of possible mass starvation.

Although far from modest when engaged in intellectual intercourse (indeed, he seemed quite egotistical at times), his unwillingness to appreciate fully the light that his life shed on history was characteristic of a deeper modesty. Even after repeated urgings from friends and colleagues to do his "memoirs," what he left behind on paper did not describe a whole life. Therefore, this volume is a combined autobiography-biography. Virtually all of the incomplete memoirs are reproduced here (and he would have fought even our occasional removal of parentheses or addition of a comma), with the gaps filled in largely with information gleaned from letters and interviews with his family, friends, and colleagues.

Jasny's credo could not have been better stated than it was in the 1949 dedication of his Agricultural volume: "To those in Soviet Russia—far away and yet so near—who believe in science, unadorned and unadulterated science; statistics, simply factual statistics; plain truth, untarnished and unvarnished."

The authors wish to thank the members of Jasny's family for their interest, assistance, and patience in the preparation of this book; Dr. J. H. Richter and Mrs. Luba Richter for their contributions to Part 3 and to the bibliography; Jack Miller for the donation of his collection of letters and notes; the many colleagues and friends who generously contributed their recollections and impressions; and, finally, Darlene Heacock for her excellent typing and encouragement.

In the pages that follow, the footnotes are Jasny's, whereas the notes at the back of the book are the Lairds'. Although Jasny's writings have been adhered to very closely, some minor stylistic changes (especially with regard to capitalization) have been made.

Contents

Part I

RUSSIA: GROWING UP IN A REVOLUTIONARY ERA

1—The Family and Schooling

CHILDHOOD

I was born in Kharkov, Ukraine, on January 25 (old calendar)[1] 1883, the son of a well-to-do Jewish businessman. The family was split. I was one of my mother's favorites. The subdivision was important. My father being one hundred per cent a businessman and my being in the opposing camp may have something to do with the fact that I never had any liking for business.

Thus, in his incomplete autobiography, Naum Mikhailovich Jasny dismisses the first eight years of his life. Naum was the second of six children, but the first boy, born to Michael Abramovich Jasny and his wife, Rosa. The first-born was Sonya (1881), followed by Naum and four brothers—Alexander (1884), Simon (1886), Vladimir (1889), and Lev (1891).

Michael Jasny had moved to Kharkov from the small town of Zolotonosha on the Dnepr (Cherkasa Province), where he had studied to become a rabbi. Obtaining permission to leave the Pale of Settlement, Michael abandoned the idea of a religious life, and with his wife and his two brothers established a flour-milling business in the city. Under Michael's management, the mill was almost immediately a success; for its owner, we are told, was endowed with extraordinary energy, ambition, and imagination. Quickly expanding his operation, he used the mill as a stepping stone towards new opportunities. His astuteness in money matters gained him valuable contacts in the business world, and his handsome face, figure, and vivacious personality did not go unnoticed by the ladies. Despite his joie de vivre, Michael seems to have been a business genius. Turning to gold everything that he touched, this industrial Midas amassed considerable wealth and eventually came to be classified as a Third Guild merchant.[2] Expanding into the realm of chemicals, he established the Livengoskaya factories (Livengoskaya Aktsinegnaya Obshchestvo) in Livenhoff, and in the Donbas region he constructed an entire city, organized around and allied to one of his factories.

One is surprised to learn that Michael, who was known as a connoisseur of beautiful women, selected as his wife a quiet, dignified, plain (some even said "homely") Ukrainian woman. Rosalya Evlevna Poyurovskaya had come from the small city of Kremenchug, also on the Dnepr, southeast of Michael's birthplace, Zolotonosha.

While Michael sought numerous outlets for his boundless energy, Rosa apparently was content with minding the children and managing their spacious Kharkov home and the numerous servants. Generous and compassionate by nature, she willingly listened to the misfortunes of her many friends and acquaintances, who, finding a sympathetic ear, took advantage of her benevolence. Indeed, although Michael's wife was never known for physical beauty, her reputation for generosity and understanding was widespread.

However solicitous Rosa was toward her compeers, her family came first. Although not an intellectual herself, Rosa wanted her children to have the best education that could be provided. Rather than dispatch them to a grammar school, she employed private tutors, including a German governess who would teach them a second language. In order to enrich their routine instruction, she engaged a music teacher, who, along with his small daughter, moved, baggage and instruments, into the Jasny household. Rosa bustled about, looking after him almost as she looked after her own children, fretting because he neglected to change his underwear. Her efforts were rewarded to the extent that Naum became an avid Wagnerian fan, and at least Volodya (Vladimir) learned to play the violin. Believing that her children should be provided with opportunities to meet celebrities, Rosa, without consulting Michael, invited a noted French diplomat to call at their home. It was an occasion long remembered by the children, for their distinguished guest entertained them with stories of Paris, leaving them wide-eyed with one account of a restaurant in which the customers were served by nude waitresses.

Religion in the Jasny family was never emphasized, for even though at one time Michael had planned to become a rabbi, in later years he relegated religion to a minor position in his crowded life. Once or twice a year he attended the synagogue, but he did not encourage worship by the children beyond the observation of important religious holidays and the celebration of these holidays with traditional foods.

In Michael's busy existence there was little time for the children, and it is small wonder that his eldest son developed a strong preference for his mother. Certainly Michael, with his extraordinary talents and persistence, must have been an impossible figure for his sons to strive to emulate. Indeed, the entire family lived in his shadow, admiring and respecting him and hoping that some day, perhaps, Alexander, who seemed to have inherited the greatest potential, would follow in his father's footsteps, however far behind. No one appeared to recognize that it was Naum who possessed the same qualities of intelligence, curiosity, ambition, and persistence that impelled his father to achievement in the business world. Certainly Naum repudiated his father's interests, and with the encouragement of his mother and Sonya, whom he greatly admired and who taught him to love literature, he sought his niche in the intellectual sphere.

Naum's brothers regarded him as "independent," somewhat "apart" (as Simon recalls) from the rest of the family, surely not very promising since he rejected all that his illustrious father held important. Rosa's encouraging of Naum in the world of letters opened to the boy a domain which was not dominated by Michael's genius, an area in which Naum could prove to his father that he was more than just his "good-for-nothing offspring"—a term used by Naum.

THE GYMNASIUM

At the age of nine, Naum was enrolled in a gymnasium and exposed to the traditional classical education.

My father pushed me into a classical gymnasium when I was underage. Fortunately I had to spend two years in the fifth grade (there was a total of eight grades, finishing at eighteen as the youngest). About one-third of the school time was devoted to classical languages, for which I did not have either ability or interest. (I made some slight use of my small familiarity with classical languages when

When I was in the sixth grade (I was just over sixteen at the time) an inter-school organization for self-education along revolutionary lines was started in the town. It was influenced by the local Social-Democrats. Made up of some fifteen boys and girls from five or six schools, the organization was of course secret and was indeed a very rare phenomenon for that time (even the abortive revolution of 1905 was six or seven years away). Unfortunately, there was too much drinking. There were also several unstable participants: one of them committed suicide; another, who played a considerable role in the organization, completely deteriorated morally. The organization operated fully only during that one year, but most of the contacts were kept.

In spite of the beneficial effect the organization and its contacts had on me (the attachment to drink I shook off soon afterwards), I was very immature even for my eighteen years when I graduated from the gymnasium in 1901.

THE UNIVERSITY

Since he did not get a gold medal, Naum was forced to choose a university outside of Russia, and in the fall of 1901 he enrolled in chemistry at the University of Berlin. The following year the law was changed briefly, allowing Jews without the gold medal to enter Russian universities, and Naum returned to his home town.

In 1902 I returned to Kharkov and shifted to law, as I believed it was the field that would most easily leave me much time for the revolutionary activities I intended to engage in. In 1904 I went to Vienna and then to Zurich, because I was expelled from Kharkov University for alleged political activities without the right ever again to enter a Russian university.

I was not too interested in most of the subjects studied at the universities (so far as Russian universities were concerned, the courses were prescribed). So let me conclude this part by saying a few words about examinations. Seminars not yet having been introduced, the examinations provided the only contacts students had with their professors. I do not like exams, because I hate to be asked questions the answers to which depend on the inquiry, "What questions is the professor asking, and what answers does he expect to get?"

Among the examinations in my first or second year was statistics.

The prescribed text was by Chuprov, not the internationally known Alexander Chuprov, but his father. In Russia, he was perhaps even more prominent than his son, but his text did not contain anything of interest on statistics. It was a reference book, supposed to be memorized, on what kind, during which periods, and how censuses were to be taken, and similar information. Not being able to overcome the aversion to such material, I procured a translation of an American text and, after studying it, dared to present myself for an examination to Professor A. Antsiferov, well known not only as a statistician but also as a cooperator. I fared well enough in the exam until finally the professor began to realize that I was unfamiliar with the prescribed textbook. So he said, "I can see that you understand statistical theory well, but you do not apparently know some important details. I very much want to give you the mark Excellent, but I must continue the examination." My answer came naturally, "If the question is only between Excellent and Satisfactory, do permit me to leave." So saying, I got up and, since the professor remained silent, tactfully left. Several years later, when I received my parting papers from the university, I found that Professor Antsiferov after all had given me the mark Excellent.

In 1904, while Naum was attending school outside of Russia, Michael Jasny shifted his base of operations to St. Petersburg, where he moved his family into a magnificent top-floor apartment, which had two sitting rooms, a study, ten bedrooms, a huge formal dining room, a kitchen, and servants' quarters. Michael, however, not being entirely satisfied, ordered one of the sitting rooms to be redecorated in Louis XVI style. Elegant with gold and glass, the room was ever after known as the Louis Seize room, a chamber in which awe-struck grandchildren were permitted to gaze at the procelain delicacies in the corner glass cabinet, but never to touch them.

POLITICS VERSUS STUDY

When the famous march of St. Petersburg workers to the tsar's palace, under the leadership of the priest Gapon, took place in January, 1905, I decided that this was no time for study, that it was necessary to return to Russia to help in the overthrowing of tsarism. Until October or November of the same year I was in the St. Petersburg organization of the Mensheviks, acting as a propagandist and organizer. I was successful so far as political analysis was involved, but some difficulties resulted from my not being too good in contacts with people. In the late fall I had a very difficult attack of typhoid with complications. The illness and convalescence took up all winter (the illness prevented my arrest, incidentally).

With this brief paragraph, Jasny dismisses what must have been an intriguing year. Unfortunately, we can add only one incident to his account, one which Jasny himself related to Professor Alec Nove (University of Glasgow), which apparently took place in late April and early May of 1905, when Jasny was sent to Warsaw to organize a May Day demonstration. According to his account, he accomplished his assignment successfully (avoiding the police) and decided to go for a Saturday stroll about the Jewish quarter of the city. Expecting the inhabitants to be friendly and receptive, he was completely bewildered when, instead, they cursed and threatened him and even kicked at him in the street. Upon asking someone why he was so poorly received by his own people, he learned to his embarrassment that he had committed the grievous error of smoking in public on the Sabbath.

Since almost nothing is said of my political activities in these memoirs, they may be briefly sketched here. The year 1905 turned out to be the only period in which I have devoted all or even much of my time to politics. In 1906, after I entered St. Petersburg University (the ban against Jews had been voided by the abortive revolution of 1905), we had for some time regular meetings of a small, highly educated group (I certainly was the dumbest). While all the participants were Marxists (mostly Mensheviks), participation in these meetings could hardly be considered political activity. It is of interest that nearly everybody in the group made something of himself. One young man, who had been with me at the gymnasium, eventually became a professor at Petrograd University, inheriting the chair of the famous M. M. Kovalevski; another became a prominent legal writer; still another made a name as a professor of labor economics. My career, for what it is worth, is described here. But the one who seemed the ablest, indeed the only brilliant one among us, fared worst. He spent his university years jumping from subject to subject and had nothing else to do after completing his studies at the university than to become a lawyer, for which he had no heart. So his career was nothing to brag about.

Thereafter I drifted away from politics entirely until the Revolution. After my return to Kharkov at the end of 1917 and later in Tiflis (now Tbilisi), I was active as a writer for Menshevik publications. There was an interruption in my political contacts until about 1925 or 1928, when my friend Peter Garvy, the leader of the right-wing Mensheviks, persuaded me to become active in the Menshevik organization in Berlin. This continued also afterwards in the U.S.A., but my participation was limited to publication of articles on economic subjects in the Menshevik journal and to giving talks on the same topics.

On the whole, for a long time it had been clear to me and to the Menshevik leaders, with whom I had been on good terms, that I was not made of the right meat for political activity. In subsequent years I realized that organizational work, propaganda, and everything else connected with active party work just does not agree with my inclinations as an individualist and fighter for the truth.

As one prominent Menshevik told me, "With reference to everybody else it is possible to predict the position he will take on this or the other problem. But you are unpredictable."

As should be obvious from this account, my connections were only with the Menshevik wing of the Social-Democrats (I was undecided between Bolsheviks and Mensheviks only until Lenin published in 1904 his *One Step Forward, Two Steps Back* which seemed to me to be syndicalism, Bonapartism, anything but social-democratism). Whatever little political activity I was ever involved in was confined to the Mensheviks; I never had any connections with any other party. Within the Mensheviks, who had an inclination toward splitting into factions, I refused to take sides, and after the 1905 uprising, my connections even with them became very loose.

Although by as early as 1904 in Vienna I had begun to feel acutely my lack of ability for thorough study, for acquiring serious, real knowledge, it was not until 1907 that I fully recognized the problem. In St. Petersburg University, examinations were conducted much more seriously than in Kharkov. I passed a few of them (with the exception of Church Law) with the mark Excellent, but then it happened. In the spring of 1907 I took an exam in criminal law with Professor Zhizhilenko, and he did not let me pass. He did not ask me out-of-the-way questions, as one of his colleagues did. He proved to my satisfaction that my knowledge was superficial, that I did not really understand the basic concepts of the subject. I was crushed.

I had not prepared for the exam in criminal law any less than I had for the other subjects. Therefore, I had to conclude that I was incapable of acquiring real knowledge.

But I did not give up. For seven months I studied criminal and Roman civil law from early in the morning till late at night for the exams which would be offered again in December. I hardly slept the last nights and did not sleep at all the very last night before the exam in criminal law. I felt relieved only after I listened to the questions and answers of a few students whose turn in the exam came before mine. When I realized that I could answer every question properly, I went into the hall for the first pleasant smoke in seven months of uncertainty. I almost forgot to mention that I got the mark Excellent both in criminal law and, two weeks later, in Roman civil law.

The more time that has passed since that occasion, the clearer it has become that research is the only suitable occupation for me, and the stronger has become the realization that to some extent I am indebted to Professor Zhizhilenko for my success.

I finished the university in 1908 with a diploma of first degree and fourteen Excellent marks out of seventeen (I needed only nine) —this shows how easy it had been. My thesis on business cycles (largely a formality, I believe) was approved.

Meanwhile, Michael Jasny's empire had been growing; he had added a brick factory in Moscow and a glass factory in St. Petersburg. Rosa, however, apparently felt that his interests were too narrow, for when a gentleman from the Popov Publishing House approached her with the proposition that the Jasnys buy it and employ him as manager, she seemed delighted with the idea and suggested it to Michael. Her husband was dumbfounded; "What do I want with a publishing house?" he demanded.

Rosa applied feminine pressure, "You buy everything else," she is reported to have said, "a factory here and a factory there, but when a good man comes along and offers you something like this, you are not interested."

Acknowledging defeat, Michael bought the publishing house, installing the "good man" as manager. Then, typically, he purchased a bookstore on Nevski prospekt, as an outlet, and a paper company to supply materials. Unfortunately, the "good man" proved dishonest, and management of the publishing house fell to the Jasny family. Simya (Simon), having graduated from the University of St.

Petersburg, was the first to try it; but reflecting his father's tastes, he found it not to his liking. After a few months, Vladimir—the only son not to finish high school and attend a university—assumed control and, to Rosa's delight, made a successful business of her pet project.

Volodya's outgoing personality was well suited to the publishing business, for he made friends easily. Among his acquaintances he counted Roman Jakobson, a younger cousin with a growing propensity for linguistics, and Vladimir Mayakovsky, the writer who shocked the Jasnys at one of their receptions with his appalling manners, as he casually tossed bones from the chicken he was eating over his shoulder onto the floor.

RESPONSIBILITIES

After graduating from St. Petersburg University, Naum Jasny wanted nothing to do with the growing Jasny enterprises, and in fact, he encouraged the rancor of his family by falling in love with and wanting to marry a young lady from the lower nobility of Nizhny Novgorod (now Gorki), Mariya Vasilevna Orlova. Mariya, the daughter of a doctor in government employ, was an intelligent, handsome, and energetic young woman who, in spite of having been educated in a school for the nobility, shared Naum's enthusiasm for a socialist revolution, although she was never as active as he.

Strong family opposition on both sides was only the first obstacle placed in the path of the courtship. In the second place, Mariya, who planned to become a doctor, was attending medical school at Moscow University, and Jasny, a Jew, was not permitted to travel to Moscow. In the third place, not only was Mariya a gentile, but since she was a member of the Russian Orthodox Church, she could not marry a Jew, who was considered two levels below her on the religious-social scale (there were no civil marriages, only those sanctified by the Church). Confronted with these difficulties, most couples would surely have accepted defeat, but Naum and Mariya were not to be thwarted, and Jasny persistence and imagination were applied to the problem. Obtaining a false passport, Naum, in spite of the danger, carried on the courtship in Moscow, where Mariya, learning with dismay that she fainted too easily, gave up becoming a doctor and accepted a dental degree instead. She then officially renounced her religion, becoming a Protestant so that she could legally marry a Jew. This must have constituted a considerable sacrifice for Mariya, since she was deeply religious. Braving family opposition, the couple were married, and on June 11, 1909 (New Calendar), their first child, Natalie (called Natascha), was born, an event which quickly silenced any remaining family opposition.

Mariya proved to be an excellent wife and mother. Not naturally aggressive, she let her ambitious husband take the lead, supporting him in his interests and activities, and even giving up her church attendance at his request. Her honesty, dignity, gentleness, and kindness endeared her to her husband and children, and her ability in later years to adapt uncomplainingly from a life of wealth and ease to the bare existence of extreme poverty in a foreign country, and even to devastating illness, gained her their undying devotion.

But now, Naum Jasny found himself saddled with the responsibility of a family and further encumbered by the many arbitrary restrictions against Jews wishing to practice law.

All a Jew was permitted to do in the legal profession was to become a lawyer. I tried it. I was not a complete failure.

Another lawyer submitted to the Supreme Court a paper which I had written on a rather difficult case involving Bessarabian (Moldavian) law. But I had only a few law cases of my own, and none with payment. I simply did not know how to attract clients (a lawyer correctly diagnosed the situation when he said to me: "You'd better give it up; you will never have a client"). In the meantime I had married, and a baby was expected. So I had no choice but to become manager in my father's flour mill. This meant, in effect, becoming a partner in a business that was then making a loss.

I did well so far as technical direction of the flour mill and the purchase of the grain for it were concerned. The selling of flour, my weak point, was handled by others. So I succeeded in converting losses into profits. But I was not happy in the business. Soon after World War I started, the disturbances in the grain markets brought in such a flood of profits that I felt like a robber. In 1916 I left Kharkov and accepted a job in Pskov with the Union of Cities.

2—Finding His Way: Groman

The following section, left in its original form, describes in detail what Naum Jasny thought of as the Groman era of his life, a period beginning just before the overthrow of the tsarist government and ending just after it. This chapter is especially interesting, in that it elaborates some of the extraordinary problems confronting the Provisional Government, and eventually the Bolsheviks, and reveals early efforts to establish the planned regulation of the economy.

The Union of Cities, like the armed forces themselves, was divided into three fronts, the northern, the central, and the southern. The center of our organization for the northern front was in Pskov, where we looked after fugitives from the fighting areas, providing them with food and medical care. I was in charge of the food branch there, but my inability to handle people caused difficulties. While I was not dropped, I myself felt that the job did not suit me or, what amounts to the same thing, that I was not suitable for the job. I tried to transfer to the central organization in Moscow, where there was a branch of the Union in charge of procurements of food for all three sections of the front. It was headed by Vladimir Ivanovich Astrov. I suggested to him that the branch would profit by having sections for the principal commodities and offered my services for the section dealing with grain products, where my familiarity with the products would have been useful. V. Astrov refused my offer.*

---

* Some weeks later, after a conference on the organization of flour milling (which is discussed below), V. Astrov confessed, "I am sorry that I did not

Feeling very dissatisfied with the Pskov job, for the first and last time in my life I resorted to asking for an introduction. I received it from Nikolai Vasilievich Teslenko, a well-known lawyer and a prominent member of the State Duma from the Kadet party. The introduction was to Nikolai Ivanovich Astrov (brother of Vladimir), the brilliant, extremely well mannered head of the Union of Cities, one of the two most influential quasi-governmental central organizations of that time.* N. I. Astrov, also head of the economic division of the same Union, had never through introduction hired a satisfactory employee, and so, hoping to discourage me, he offered me the modest position of assistant secretary in his personal secretariat. However, wanting desperately not to leave the Union of Cities, my first connection with an organization of this kind, I surprised Astrov by accepting his offer. The secretariat was headed by Mark Venyaminovich Vishnyak, soon to become secretary of the Constituent Assembly. Lev Nikolayevich Litoshenko, a young but well-known economist, acted as adviser and edited the journal published by the Union.

My own position was a very small one. A campaign was in progress just then to induce the government to revise the laws pertaining to the organization of the city governments, the so-called City Status. The campaign was conducted by the Union of Cities, actually by N. I. Astrov. A series of meetings and conferences took place in rapid succession, and I was hired to prepare the minutes. The only difficulty I experienced was that while most participants, well-known personalities, were familiar to me, I knew most of them only by their last names, but in the meetings they were referred to, as was customary, by their first and patronymic names. Astrov, having been fully satisfied with my work, assigned me to discuss the desired revisions of the City Status in the journal published by the Union of Cities. That article was my first. I was thirty-three years old.

Sometime during the summer of 1916 (probably early in July), the door of the secretariat was torn open, and a heavy man burst in. It was Vladimir Gustavovich Groman. I mentioned above that N. I.

---

accept your suggestion then. I just thought that you were finding life in Pskov boring. I understand that now you would not accept the job suggested by you then, but possibly you could recommend somebody for the position suggested by you."

* By quasi-governmental organizations I mean private organizations which came into being to fulfill essential functions of a governmental nature that were neglected by the autocratic political regime.

Astrov was well mannered; this was done only in view of the immense contrast with Groman, who was not anything of the kind.

Groman was about forty years old then, and he looked back over twenty years of revolutionary and statistical work. Jail and exile had taken turns with statistical jobs; in Vyatka [Kirov] both were combined. Groman apparently never played a great role as a political leader, but he did in statistical work, specifically in the famous zemstvo [provincial council] statistics. He was very successful even before fate brought him together with the brilliant economist and philosopher Alexander Bogdanov, for years second only to Lenin in the Bolshevik party. From Bogdanov, Groman acquired the idea of the economic whole. While Bogdanov himself was apparently unsuccessful in finding practical utilization for his idea, Groman successfully applied it first in his statistical, and later in his economic, work.

It turned out quite providential that soon after the beginning of World War I Groman became possessed with the necessity to fight the monetary inflation that was obviously imminent under the then-existing conditions. (From October 1, 1920, to October 1, 1922, the cost of living rose in paper money by more than 69,000 times.)* So he left a job in Penza, hurried to Moscow, and persuaded the Chuprov Society of the importance of his idea. The society and apparently some other organizations provided modest funds, and Groman issued three volumes of *Works of the Commission for the Study of the Present High Cost of Living*, published by the Chuprov Society, Moscow, 1915. But wider horizons soon opened up for him and, as it turned out, for me.

In conducting World War I, the feeble Rasputin-guided or Rasputin-influenced tsarist government made the huge error of having an excessively large army. There were not enough rifles to train all the men mobilized. Although Russia was an exporter of food and especially grain on a very large scale right up to the war, difficulties in feeding the armed forces were soon felt. Inadequate means of transportation was not the least of the causes. Not only the Siberian supplies but even those from southern and southeastern European Russia remained unused for this reason, while supplies from the more centrally located sources proved increasingly inadequate.

The Ministry of Agriculture took charge of food supplies at the

---

* *The National Economy of Russia 1921/22* (Moscow, 1923), p. 231.

outset of the war, first only for the army and later also for the civilian population. There were two organizations in Petrograd for the specific task of providing the food, those of the High Commissioner for Grain and Fodder Purchases and the High Commissioner for Meat, Fish, and Vegetable Purchases—both part of the Ministry of Agriculture. The high commissioners had their special separate apparatuses, which included commissioners in the various parts of the country. The Department of Agriculture having been relatively liberal, the Polytechnical Institute (a big university organized by the great Finance Minister Witte) or Peter Struve personally was asked to recommend suitable persons for the responsible jobs. At least four persons were so recommended, Demosfenov, Dolinski, Zaitzev, and Bukhspan, all of them certainly able persons. Bukhspan was used mainly as a journalist, Zaitzev became head of the sugar section, and Demosfenov and Dolinski went into the grain section. All of them, except apparently Bukhspan, became émigrés after the Bolshevik revolution, unfortunately landing in Prague and Bulgaria. This affected unfavorably the symposium *Food Supply in Russia during the World War* by K. I. Zaitzev, N. V. Dolinski, and S. S. Demosfenov, under the general direction of P. B. Struve in the Carnegie series devoted to the war (New Haven, 1930). I had little contact with Zaitzev, but I knew Demosfenov and Dolinski well and always felt friendly toward them. I am sure, however, that they considered people who, like Groman, stayed behind in Russia and tried to do constructive work under the Bolsheviks to be traitors. (They certainly were not alone in this attitude.) This prevented them from presenting Groman's work in the light it deserved. At least this seems so to me.*

---

* An unbiased presentation of the food situation during World War I can be found in N. D. Kondratiev, *The Grain Market and Its Regulation during the War and Revolution* (Moscow, 1922). This is the Kondratiev who is famous outside the U.S.S.R. for his 'long waves,' or long-term repetitive trends, of economic activity, the founder and director of the Konjunktur (Economic Research) Institute, adviser to the Commissariats for Agriculture and Finance, and the leader of the Neo-Narodniki in the 1920s until his disappearance after the Menshevik trial in March, 1931. I am sorry to say that in this trial Kondratiev was a witness for the prosecution. However, a study of his testimony makes it very probable that he had an agreement with the prosecution to testify only against the Mensheviks, who anyway testified against themselves. Moreover, while testifying in the first place against Groman, Kondratiev insisted on using the full first, patronymic, and last names—Vladimir Gustavo-

The difficulties in the economy compelled the tsarist government to organize in mid 1915 four Special Councils at certain ministries, including the Ministry of Agriculture. The Special Councils
were to have only consultative power. But at least the Special Council
on Food Supply at the Ministry of Agriculture (its first meeting was
on August 31, 1915) carried great weight. The councils consisted of
a relatively large number of representatives of the various government
agencies. But at least in the Special Council for Food, there were
also two representatives of the so-called social element (obshchest-
vennost), one from the Union of Zemstvos and the other from the
Union of Cities.* The well-known economist Peter Berngardovich
Struve became the representative of the Union of Zemstvos in the
Special Council for Food. Astrov showed great wisdom when he had
Groman, so diametrically different from him, appointed as the representative of the Union of Cities in the same Council.

With immense enthusiasm Groman threw himself into this new
task. Seeing the need for an immense amount of new statistics, he
persuaded Astrov to provide him with the necessary staff. (If Groman
had been given a free hand, nobody would have been doing anything
but collecting and processing statistics.) Two statistical bureaus were
organized within the economic division of the Union of Cities, one
in Moscow and the other in Petrograd. The Moscow bureau, headed
by Pavel Ilich Popov as Groman's deputy chief, was engaged in work
of long standing (this is the same Popov who later, under the Bolshe-

---

vich Groman—every time he mentioned Groman. This makes a great impression—even now in reading. It must have acted as a demonstration when again
and again done orally in court. Kondratiev seems to have been far from having
been broken at that time, I am happy to say. The official allegedly verbatim
('stenographic') report on the Menshevik trial in which Groman was the star
accused (the report is available in the U.S. Library of Congress) has apparently
never been subjected to a careful scrutiny. It may possibly give support to a
rumor that there was at least one other agreement with the prosecution. I
heard it ascribed to Nikolai Nikolayevich Sukhanov, mentioned in the second
piece of these memoirs, that for the false testimony desired by the prosecution,
the accused were promised not only freedom but return to their previous occu-
pations. If this be true, the accused too were less broken than one might
think they were.

* Zemstvos were the governments of the gubernii (now oblasts), except
that the large cities were excluded from their competence. These had their
own dumas and city heads. For good reasons the zemstvos were much more
liberal than the city municipalities. But the Union of Cities was at least as
liberal as the Union of Zemstvos.

viks, was head of the Central Statistical Office for several years). The Petrograd bureau was engaged primarily in current problems, being intended specifically to assist Groman in his day-to-day work as representative in the Special Council for Food. The friendly Fedor Andreyevich Cherevanin (born Lipkin), a prominent old Menshevik, known also for his work in economics, was deputy chief there. Whereas the Moscow office had a large staff, the personnel of the Petrograd bureau consisted of five or six "statisticians" (analysts), seven or eight "assistant statisticians," and one secretary. (The chief of the assistant statisticians, who operated as a group, was a lady by the name of Adamovich, an openly enthusiastic Bolshevik. Her assistant was no less a person than Mariya Ilinishna Ulyanova, Lenin's sister.)

In pursuit of his work in the Special Council, Groman succeeded in having a decision passed by the council that a survey of the flour-milling industry be carried out. Groman felt that he should present to the council a questionnaire for the mills participating in the survey, and ordered a small conference to be called in Moscow, consisting of prominent economists and statisticians, to work out the questionnaire.

Groman knew nothing of flour milling; and having been told that there was someone in Astrov's secretariat who was knowledgeable on the subject, he stormed into our office, demanding to know who that man was. Upon being informed that I was that person, he announced that a conference on the flour-milling survey was to take place that very day and that he wanted me for the rather modest task of preparing the minutes.

This was the first time that I had ever seen Groman, in spite of the fact that his Moscow bureau was next to our office. All I knew about him was that Astrov and Vishnyak spoke of him with great respect, respect mingled with considerable reserve, perhaps even some fear. The only person I knew in his office was the wife of Vladimir Osipovich Levitski (brother of the famous Menshevik leader Martov, and a friend of mine). She spoke of Groman with greater awe than I have ever heard before or since. As it turned out, this attitude was common among Groman's collaborators, for Groman had an unusual ability to attract devoted assistants. He lighted in them a religious zeal towards their work, however ordinary. Some of his assistants from Penza, where he had headed a *zemstvo guberniya* statistical office, followed him in his subsequent activities until the very end of his active life.

When the conference convened, it turned out that, however

deserving they may have been of their great reputations, not one of those present had ever been in a flour mill or had the slightest understanding of the milling process. It was only natural, therefore, that in addition to preparing the minutes of the meeting, I should also draft the questionnaire. This small feat threw Groman into a state of wild enthusiasm. The very next morning he went to Astrov and demanded my transfer to his bureau under threat of resignation. Astrov was unwilling but felt he had to comply. A new page was turned in my life, the first page of my scientific career.

Groman placed me in his Petrograd bureau. Officially I was one of the "statisticians," but actually had a higher position, possibly immediately under Groman himself. The most important thing was that Groman gave me a tremendous opportunity and treated me as though I were a great scholar.

As already said, the work in the bureau concentrated around the work of the Central Food Council. Groman continued his fight against high prices in this also. Soon after my transfer to his organization, a conference of the commissioners took place to establish the prices to be paid to producers for grain during the 1916–1917 crop year. The commissioners consisted mostly of wealthy landlords, with "your excellencies" and even princes richly strewn among them. It was fascinating to observe how Groman, in a suit which had never been pressed since he bought it off the rack, made himself heard. In spite of his immense drive, however, the commissioners decided on prices which he believed too high. Groman's continued pressure brought the army's interference in favor of his proposals.

Encountering difficulty in procuring the food, in particular the grain, needed to feed the armed forces, the local commissioners made extended use of the power given them to prohibit the use of railway wagons for shipments of grain and flour out of the *guberniya* of origin, and this led to growing shortages of food among the urban population. The areas near the war front, especially Warsaw, were most affected, but Petrograd and even Moscow also experienced difficulties. The shortages boosted prices in the private markets, thus making it difficult for the commissioners to procure supplies even for the army. Inflationary pressures increased in spite of availability at first of large supplies at the places of their production. Quite naturally, surpluses in the more distant regions led to curtailment of output. The 1916 crop year was most affected. The year 1914–1915 had still the crop of a peace year, while 1915 was a climatically favorable year.

conference, I was permitted to go ahead with it in the Central Flour Bureau. The millers engaged in a real war, calling me a traitor, among other things. The milling industry even held a special congress on the matter. A big conference took place in the Central Flour Bureau also, at which the milling industry was represented in force, including milling engineers, with me alone defending the proposal. We succeeded in putting through then only a three-grade grinding, but a few weeks later the government, on its own initiative, made the one-grade grinding obligatory.

I recall another occasion. This also happened soon after I had started to work in Groman's bureau. Groman was invited to speak in the renowned Imperial Free Economic Society, a place I thought of only with great awe. I would not have dreamed of raising my voice there. On the very day Groman was due to speak in the Society, he was preparing to leave for Moscow. On my remark that he had a speaking engagement for that evening Groman said: "You go, and let Fedor Andreyevich accompany you in case you need help." I had the pleasure of Fedor Andreyevich's company, but he did not feel that I needed help.

Groman never used an idea of mine without specifying the source. In this he went beyond reason. It was only natural that most of the memoranda which we sent to the Special Council in a flood were actually written by me, the technician, but of course the papers had to be signed by Groman, as the official representative. But Groman was unhappy. He ordered me to collect the memoranda for publication, in the preface of which the authorship of each memorandum would be stated. I found publication just for giving credit to me absurd, and sabotaged the order. It was stupid of me. While I still believe the matter of credit not worth attention, the publication of the memoranda would have been important per se. It would have made more obvious the distortions in the writings of the Belgrade-Sofia refugees in the Carnegie volume. In the Special Council, the Central Flour Bureau, and simply in our bureau, history was in the making at that time, and I did not realize it.

I worked hard, of course, during my association with Groman. The office opened at 9 A.M., and I rarely returned home before midnight, the meetings in the Central Flour Bureau frequently taking place in the evenings. I still remember how happy my wife and I were when I succeeded in getting tickets for *Don Quixote*, with Chalyapin in the title role, and then a meeting of the bureau prevented my attending. But these were minor inconveniences, for the short period of my work with Groman was by far the happiest period in my life.

It has taken much space to describe the period of my collaboration with Groman, but it lasted only about seven months, from some time in July, 1916, to February 27 (old calendar), when the power of the tsar was overthrown. Seven months only—but during this short period I found my way in life.

3—The 1917 Revolution
and the Break with Groman

THE UPRISING

Upon returning in 1916 to what had become Petrograd, Naum, Mariya,[1] and their six-year-old daughter, Natascha, had moved into the huge Jasny apartment with Naum's parents and his two youngest brothers, Vladimir and Lev. Since Alexander and Simon had married beautiful wives, to their father's delight, and were living in apartments of their own, there was more than enough room for Naum's family.

Vladimir was managing the publishing house, and Lev, barely eighteen, was a student in engineering school. The latter was a sensitive boy, and Natascha delighted in teasing her teenage uncle, much to his annoyance. In the fall of 1916—having turned seven in June—Natascha began attending a nearby grammar school, accompanied on the fifteen-minute walk to school by her nurse. Naum was keeping long hours in Groman's bureau.

February 27, 1917 (old calendar), dawned very much like the other days that week, with increasing tenseness noticeable in the streets.

The Revolution was certainly a great event for me. I had been in the antitsarist ranks since I was sixteen. Unfortunately it turned out that the overthrowing of the tsar, the great, the happy event, was also the end of collaboration with Groman, a deeply regretted occurrence, almost a calamity.

Petrograd was in a condition of great disturbance for several days prior to the fateful day. Soldiers were shooting at the crowd on Nevski prospekt, Petrograd's main street, but it was reliably reported that these were not really soldiers, the latter having refused to shoot, but policemen dressed up as soldiers. On one of those days very shortly before February 27, I stood in a doorway on Nevski prospekt (one kept in a doorway to avoid the bullets). The street was absolutely empty. It certainly looked grave for the tsarist regime. And yet it would be untrue to say that I knew the days of the tsar were numbered. In October, 1905, the situation had also been bad for the regime, but somehow getting out of the pinch, it had survived for another eleven years.

It so happened that my brother Simon had an apartment on the sixth or seventh floor on one of the Rozhdestvenskaya streets (all of them together formed the Peski, or Sands, District). Early on February 27 he called to tell us not to let our daughter Natascha go to school, which was near his house. An uprising was going on in the yard of the barracks.

Simon's telephone call that fateful morning came somewhat late, for Natascha had already left with her nurse for school. Upon receiving the message, Mariya, we are told, was horrified. Throwing on her coat, she rushed out, hoping to overtake Natascha and the nurse in the street. Unfortunately, they had too great a start, and Mariya was compelled to go the entire way to the school for her daughter. By the time she arrived, fifteen minutes later, the streets were becoming dangerous from sniper fire. Quickly withdrawing Natascha from school, she and the bewildered child started for home. They were greeted by a barrage of bullets. During the next two hours they threaded their way cautiously towards home, scurrying from one doorway to the next while rooftop snipers were reloading their machine guns. Anything that moved in the street was considered fair game.

The street, however, was not the only dangerous place. Apartment windows could be hazardous too, as Simon's wife soon discovered. Watching the street activities from an upper window, she provided an irresistible target for a nearby sniper. Fortunately, her wound was relatively minor. Lev, also, experienced a close call, but in a dissimilar way. Dressed in his engineering student's uniform, he stood at the big corner window in his father's study, excitedly surveying the street below. Army officers, or, as the rumor had it, police-

men dressed in army officers' uniforms, were seen firing into the crowds, and clusters of angry citizens and policemen were trying to locate the snipers and apprehend them. Bullets ricocheting high off the Jasny apartment building seemed to observers to be coming from the Jasny apartment. Looking up, bystanders discerned the uniformed figure of Lev standing at the window; and assuming that he was an officer who had perpetrated the shooting, they surged upstairs to arrest him. Upon invading the apartment, however, they recognized Lev's uniform as that of a student and not an officer, and their anger cooled. The crowd departed, satisfied that Lev was innocent. However, they left behind the intense anxiety which their intrusion had brought into the life of seven-year-old Natascha who, after having been fired upon in the streets only shortly before, watched, terrified, as her young uncle was threatened in his own home by strangers.

Natascha stayed home that day, but I rushed out. There was only about ten to fifteen minute's walk to the barracks. When I arrived, the soldiers were already pouring out into the street, shouting revolutionary slogans and occasionally shooting into the air. They formed an imposing procession, which moved from barracks to barracks, shouting, "Comrades, join!" And the comrades willingly joined the crowd, which consisted mostly of soldiers and was growing like an avalanche.

After a couple of hours of marching in this procession without seeing even a trace of resistance, I realized that the fate of the tsarist regime was settled, that this was not just an uprising. This was the Revolution. It seemed proper at that point for me to think of some constructive work. Since I had not yet heard about the role that the Tauride Palace was to play in the Revolution, I directed my steps to our office. There I was informed that Groman had left for the Tauride Palace and wanted everybody to stay in the office and await his directions. We waited for a couple of hours, but then when the excitement became unbearable, we started to walk towards the Tauride Palace (the streetcars were not running of course, possibly had not been for days).

In the couple of hours that we had stayed inside, the town had become unrecognizable. The streets were full of people. Cars with armed soldiers in great numbers, many of them on the running boards, were rushing by. From time to time a soldier would shoot in the air. There was also some, but not much, shooting by policemen concealed in the attics of tall houses.

Arriving finally at the palace, we were greeted by quite a sight: having been beseiged by soldiers en masse who were there not only with their ammunition but also with their food supplies, kitchens, etc., the palace was so jammed that it was not possible to move at more than a snail's pace. It must have been evening when we finally found Groman.

Deputies from factories had been arriving all the time, so that shortly Chkheidze could open the first Session of the Soviet of Workers' Deputies (renamed Soviet of Workers' and Soldiers' Deputies). If I remember correctly, the first to speak was Groman. He declared that the first task of the new government was to ensure food. He suggested that a Food Commission be appointed right away, which could start work immediately. Without debate, a commission of five was named by acclamation. Since nobody in the council knew me, I was not among the five, but Groman signaled me to join. We found a room and started to work. There was no other candidate for chairman but Groman. Everybody present was declared a member.*

The first act of the Food Commission was to send an appeal to the possessors of food not to hold it back but to help the new government with as ample supplies as possible. It was sent out the same night. The next step was to tackle the problem of organizing food supplies.

After the February Revolution, the introduction of the State Monopoly of the Grain Trade was a foregone conclusion. Not a voice was raised against it in the Food Commission, although not everybody, it is true, was sincere in agreeing to it. Quite unexpectedly a great hindrance developed. It was clear and accepted by everybody in the Food Commission that the severe and rapid inflation had made the prices paid to the producers for grain, established in early September, 1916, much too low. The disorganization in the economy was, it is true, so great that it seemed virtually impossible to establish with any precision a fair level for the new prices. They would have to be set largely arbitrarily.

Grasping at this difficulty, Groman put forward a fantastic pro-

---

* The Commission was thereafter renamed the Food Commission of the Soviet of Workers' and Soldiers' Deputies. By adding a few representatives of the State Duma, it then became the Provisional Food Commission of the State Duma and of the Soviet of the Workers' and Soldiers' Deputies, where the first crucial decisions were made.

— 29 —

posal in the Food Commission of the State Duma and of the Soviet of Workers' and Soldiers' Deputies. Since it was impossible to establish exactly the fair prices due to the producers, they were to be provisionally paid the old prices, and in addition to this they were to be given certificates. A committee was to be set up for the purpose of preparing a "Single Plan of Regulating the National Economy and Labor," and unbelievable as it seemed even then, the plan was to be completed in a matter of six weeks. It would include the exactly calculated prices to be paid to the grain producers who would then receive cash against their certificates.

Groman's ideas about planning were very much influenced by the German so-called War Communism. Nobody could have been more enthusiastic than he was. Groman did not know any foreign languages, and he would not have had time to go to primary sources even if he had known German. His sources were the articles by Yu. Lurye (later Larin) in the highly esteemed liberal Moscow daily *Russikye vedomosti*, which certainly played a fatal role by publishing the reports of such an unrestrained man as Lurye. After the Revolution, Larin, who in the meantime had become a left-wing Communist, was for years in the foreground with his activities in matters of the economy, and specifically planning, without distinguishing himself with anything like a realistic approach. Even Lenin, in his April 21, 1921, article on planning in *Pravda*, included Larin among the fantasists.

THE BREAK

Groman's proposal to settle the problem of prices to be paid by the state for the grain deliveries was fought bitterly in the commission from two points of view. One was the impossibility of working out such a plan in the time stated, but perhaps even more stress was laid on the danger of a new government's asking for deliveries against paper. The fight in the commission was indeed primarily for and against the "certificates."

I was among Groman's most furious opponents in the Food Commission. But we fought also in private. I would shout at him: "You are absolutely lacking in a sense of reality." And he: "How dare you! For twenty years I directed statistical work on the activities and life of the peasants." And I: "You saw figures; you did not see real life." Or I: "Who will work out the Plan? I do not see the competent people." Groman's answer: "You and others" did not raise any pride in me. Or, repeatedly, Groman: "No revolution happened to Jasny;" and the latter: "I do not believe in miracles in the economy." The idea that I, less than a year out of a flour mill, would play a major role in working out the Single Plan, the first such plan in the world, in a matter of six weeks, for the largest country and one of the largest populations in the world, seemed simply appalling.

I recall one incident vividly. Groman was expounding his idea in a meeting of the Food Commission. I whispered to Cherevanin, Groman's deputy in the extinct Petrograd branch of Groman's Statistical Bureau, sitting next to me: "But he is crazy." In a nearly hysterical voice Cherevanin asked, "About whom are you speaking?" Poor Fedor Andreyevich! Every word of Groman's was the highest wisdom and infallible to him.

That Groman and I came to be in opposite camps and especially that Groman advocated something radical and I was for moderation came as a great surprise to those who knew our work in the Special Council and the Central Flour Bureau, especially to Salaskin, the chairman of the Central Flour Bureau. Salaskin repeatedly joked that Groman had circled Jasny from the left front.

Groman's "certificates" were defeated in the Food Commission by a small majority. The prices suggested by this majority, largely by the undersigned, were hastily approved; the law on the monopoly of grain trade was quickly passed through the government (the Law of March 25, 1917) and the monopoly came into operation.

From July, 1916, until the passing of the Law on the Monopoly of the Grain Trade on March 25, 1917, was the only time when anything of importance depended upon the opinions of this writer. Since then I have had an average lifetime to think over whether the opinions I held then were right. My conclusions are indefinite; I just do not know. And if it is impossible to pass a definite judgment on events which occurred almost half a century ago, who can dare to make forecasts for a longer future? The comment that those were exceptional years, months, and days carries weight, but it does not dismiss the doubts fully.

Certainly, the monopoly of the grain trade did not operate well. The principal difficulty was that more grain was needed than any procurement system could deliver. Also, inflation was growing at an ever-more-rapid pace. In September, 1916, the fight for lower grain prices conducted by Groman involved a matter of 10–15% of the price. In March, 1917, six months later, the prices paid to producers were raised by 60%—likewise after a great fight. That summer, S. N. Prokopovitch, then minister of food, doubled the same prices without even consulting the All-Union Food Board.

However, there seems to be no reason to assume that in the disturbed conditions of the time any form of a procurement organization other than the monopoly would have operated better, that indeed the situation would not have been still worse otherwise.

In the summer of 1917 Groman tried to make me join the Petrograd Central Food Organization, of which he had become the head soon after the Revolution. He had run into considerable difficulty, for the food situation in Petrograd certainly was deplorable. But it was so in the whole country. Yet the press blamed him for the small rations and other deprivations of the population. The type of work to be done also may not have suited Groman best. But I did not feel that there was much that I could do (I had failed previously on more than one occasion in organizational tasks) and decided to continue the work I was doing. However, I did write an article for Den, Potresov's daily,* on the work of the Petrograd food organization, pointing out the great difficulties it faced.

I did not see Groman again until the Spring of 1923 in Berlin, when he came to have his heart trouble treated. A famous German specialist told him he would soon die if he did not give up drinking and smoking. Groman did neither. Two years later the same doctor told him, "Go on drinking and smoking; my medicine is no good for you."

We met as friends. Almost his first words were, "You were right then." Nothing more was said, but there was not the smallest doubt that his statement referred to the fixed prices for grain, the certificates, and the Single Plan of Regulating the National Economy and Labor—all of them of March, 1917. I did not come back to the

---

* Potresov was the leader of the right-wing Mensheviks. My occasional contributions to his paper misled some to include me with the group. I let Den have the articles because before the Revolution, S. Zagorski used to come to our office and ask for contributions for the paper. There was no reason to make changes in this arrangement after the Revolution, especially since I was writing on topics which had no relation to disagreements between the factions of the Menshevik party. Groman, however, shifted to the more radical Gorki paper.

issue later either, considering it a delicate matter. But in 1961 I learned from N. V. Valentinov, who in 1923–1927 had been associate editor of the only economic daily in Moscow and was then in close contact with Groman, that the latter spoke freely of the error in planning which he had committed in 1917.

After years of preparation, it took Groman's division of the U.S.S.R. Gosplan several months in 1925 to work out the Control Figures for 1925–1926, a book small enough to slip in one's pocket, infinitely more modest than Groman's ambitious Single Plan for Regulating the National Economy and Labor to be worked out in six weeks in 1917. Even so, the "Control Figures" needed hasty repairs after only three months. Although free recognition by Groman of his 1917 error by 1923 may not seem an extraordinary feat, I know of nobody else as candid amongst those active in that period.

Groman's ability freely to acknowledge an error was indeed the reason, a decisive reason in my opinion, why he, a fanatic, indeed almost a madman, of 1917, was able a few years later to play a vital part in creating planning in the U.S.S.R. and, indeed, to become a forceful defender of moderation.* When I put in my *Essays on the Soviet Economy*, published in 1962, the motto "Through frank recognition of errors to the truth," I had in mind the attitude of both Groman and myself.

I am certainly proud to have been Groman's most important collaborator during an important period of his and my activities (for me it was the most important period; Groman would probably count the work on the *Control Figures* in 1925–1927 as the most important period of his creative life). But I am not less proud that I broke with Groman—I was the only Gromanite to do so—in spite of the great esteem I had for him, when he started to advocate a step which seemed to me not to be in the interests of the cause we both were fighting for.

Since the very start of the conflict about the "certificates" and "the Single Plan," it was clear that my good relations with Groman had come to an end. From the Union of Cities, Groman shifted to the Soviet of Workers' and Soldiers' Deputies, with a devoted personnel consisting partly of his people from Penza and partly of new acquisitions, while I stayed with the Union of Cities. I did not again

* See citations of his speeches in my *Soviet Industrialization, 1928–1952* (Chicago: University of Chicago Press, 1961), pp. 62 and others.

become a nobody, for by that time it was rather widely recognized that I could do useful work. When the All-State Food Board was organized (with broader powers) instead of the Special Council, I became one of the representatives on it from the Union of Cities. There was a curious misunderstanding in this connection. The representation of the Union of Cities was organized in this manner: half of the delegates were chosen by the right wing, while the second half was to represent the "revolutionary democracy." As a socialist, I certainly belonged to the "revolutionary democracy," but I did not like the subdivision (possibly because on the food front the Gromanites operated as such representatives). To my surprise I was informed from Moscow that I had been chosen deputy representative by the right wing. However much I hated to take time from work which I believed to be important, I at once took the night train to Moscow, where the Chief Committee of the Union of Cities was still located. There I declared that I refused to serve as representative of the right wing, that the whole subdivision was not to my liking, and that if they wanted me to continue as a representative of the Union, they would have to make me representative of the Union as a whole. The Chief Committee complied, and I returned to Petrograd the same night.

I was the only permanently active representative from the Union of Cities on the All-State Food Board. I was indeed one of the most active members of the board as a whole. What with frequent meetings of the board itself and meetings of the numerous commissions of the board, most of my days and many of my nights were occupied. I was also adviser to the Supreme Economic Council from its inception and as long as S. N. Prokopovitch was its president. I left when a rich capitalist replaced him. I was also invited to be adviser to the Grain Division of the Food Ministry, but the Bolshevik Revolution prevented the realization of this proposal made to me by the head of the division.

When I dissociated myself from Groman, I did not join any other group on the All-State Food Board. My ability to do useful work was sufficiently recognized to permit me to work independently, which I preferred. But, so far as policies are concerned, my position was close to that of the representatives of the Union of Zemstvos and of the consumers' cooperatives.

There was little time in this period for writing, although opportunities were unlimited. In addition to the article mentioned above,

I may have published others in *Den*. I wrote a brochure, *War and the Food Problem*, published by Popov, and a more comprehensive work on the same general subject for the Ministry of Food (L. N. Yurovski, later to play a great role as an expert in Soviet finance, was head of the Economic Division of the ministry and was also in charge of the publications of the ministry). Shortly after seeing the small book in galley proof, I left Petrograd for the South and was not in the North again. I do not know whether the book went through the final stages of printing.

Although I do not intend to describe in detail the events on the food front during the period of the Provisional Government, I should perhaps mention some of the many prominent persons with whom I came in contact during this period. They include N. D. Kondratiev, then very young, a man of exceptional abilities, deputy minister of food at that time, later the leader of the Neo-Narodnik group; I. A. Mikhailov, a very able but unstable (possibly excessively ambitious) man, secretary general of the Supreme Economic Council for some time in 1917, later to play a fatal role as finance minister of the Kolchak government in Siberia; A. I. Shingarev, a very able man, a brilliant speaker, who was, however, active in fields for which he lacked the necessary training (originally a medical doctor, in the Lvov-Kerenski government he was first minister of food and then minister of finance); S. N. Prokopovitch, an economist, a hard worker but not much more, in the Kerenski government president of the Supreme Economic Council (not very well suited) and later minister of food (possibly even less suited); and V. N. Zelheim, a charming man, prominent in the consumers' cooperatives movement, deputy minister of food in the Kerenski government.

It would not be right if I did not mention here an episode in which I committed what I believe to be the greatest error of my life. The inclusion of this episode is the more proper since it can well be considered the concluding act of the earliest period of the February Revolution, "concluding" at least so far as I was concerned.

In the first few days after the February Revolution it was decided that the State Duma would approve commissars to be put into the ministries inherited from the tsarist time. The Soviet of Workers' and Soldiers' Deputies was to appoint the deputy commissars. The State Duma assigned the role of commissar in that section of the Ministry of Agriculture which dealt with food supplies to its member Vostrotin, who did not, however, prove very active in this capacity.

The Soviet of Workers' and Soldiers' Deputies nominated two men, one of whom was myself, as deputy commissars in the same agency. Since the second man preferred to take on the separate part of the organization dealing with animal products, I was operating in the main part of it (the parts were separate even territorially, the respective head offices being in different buildings). When the Provisional Government was formed with A. N. Shingarev as the minister of agriculture, as before the Revolution, in charge also of procurements of food,* it looked as though he was taking over the ministry from me. In our parting conference I suggested that the first thing Shingarev had to do was to persuade the government that the amount of food procurable would not suffice to feed the huge armed forces and at least the largest cities, and that steps must be taken at once to curtail the armed forces. My suggestion put Shingarev in a state of great excitement. He declared the idea to be absolutely impossible. My big error was that I did not pursue the idea over Shingarev's head. I simply lacked the courage to stick to my conclusion. The most sensible thing would have been to speak to Groman, in spite of our torn relations. I am sure that he would have given much greater weight to my opinions on this matter than did the nightingale Shingarev, and he also would have found ways to make the government give the matter serious consideration. This might even have been quite beneficial for Groman himself, in that it would have distracted him a little from the idea of a Single Plan of Regulating the National Economy and Labor. But I do not recollect this step occurring to me. I could also have spoken of the idea in a meeting of the Food Commission of the Workers' and Soldiers' Deputies or of the All-State Food Board. Finally, I could at least have tried to publish an article. But Shingarev's strongly negative attitude frightened me into doing nothing, absolutely nothing. It was the same lack of courage of which I accuse others.

A very few months after my talk with Shingarev the problem of curtailment of the armed forces was raised by Verkhovski, then the minister of war, but the loss of time was irreparable. The armed forces were disintegrating at a fantastic rate, the soldiers being afraid that the land in their villages would be newly subdivided and that they would be neglected if not present. Railway traffic broke down under the strain of soldiers hurrying home.

---

* A special Ministry of Food (for supply of food and other essentials) was organized only by an order of the Provisional Government of May 5, 1917.

The case of the curtailment of the armed forces was only one among many problems about which nothing was done. This inaction seems to have been the main reason for the ultimate passing of power to Lenin and the Bolsheviks.

It would be insincere and indeed plain silly to say that during the Lvov-Kerenski period I knew what was to be done to put the country on a sound basis. The situation was too serious. The situation demanded action. The overdue Revolution had released forces which demanded a place in the sun. Foremost was the question of land and the peasantry. The peasants wanted, and right away, whatever land the landowners still held (they certainly greatly overestimated the amount of such land). They did not want to wait until the Social-Revolutionary party, which in a government like that of Kerenski naturally had the problem of land in its hands, could find the most just solution. And all this with the country a participant in a World War. Fate may have desired that the same war which made the Revolution possible prevented the fruits of the victory going to the Russian people.

A. F. Kerenski clearly did not strike one as a man for the tasks Russia was facing. I was therefore cool to the centers of the Menshevik and Social-Revolutionary parties, who were part of the Kerenski government. I knew definitely that the campaign for the abolition of the death penalty, to which Y. O. Martov, the leader of the left wing of the Mensheviks, seemed to have been devoting all his time, was not a thing which, even if successful, would have had a really constructive effect.*

I merely did what I could in the field in which I was active, feebly hoping that somehow the country would find its proper way. It did not find the way; at least, not in my opinion.

BOLSHEVISM

The advent of the Bolshevik coup in October of 1917 was relatively quiet as compared with the collapse of tsardom in February, but it precipitated the destruction of the Jasny empire and the disintegration of the family. Lenin's published plans to "terrorize" the capitalists, to confiscate their property, and to force them to work for the

---

* Once I saw Martov in the sidecar of a motorcycle, apparently being driven to one of his numerous speeches against the death penalty. I still hesitate to put on paper the impression he made on me then.

proletariat or go hungry forecast the imminent destruction of men like Michael Jasny.[2] Taking with them some money and a few belongings, Michael and Rosa left Petrograd for the resort town Kislovodsk in the Caucasus, where they remained a brief time in the futile hope that Bolshevism would collapse. Soon recognizing the unlikelihood of this occurrence, the senior Jasnys sailed for Constantinople, arriving eventually in Vienna, where Michael, exercising his amazing talents, began to maneuver himself into an important position in a local bank.

For some years prior to 1917 Simon had worked successfully alongside his father, gradually assuming more responsibility in the family enterprises. Now, upon Michael's departure, the entire complex fell into Simon's hands, and he, more conservative and less impulsive than his father, remained in Petrograd, stunned, confused, and bewildered by all that was happening around him, trying desperately to hold his world together.

Simon's reluctance to leave Petrograd nearly cost him his life, for as the director of an industrial complex he was a specified target for Bolshevik ire. House-to-house searches provided a steady flow of capitalist scapegoats who were quickly arrested, summarily tried, and shot. It was only a matter of time till Simon should fall victim to these raids. Indeed, very shortly he was arrested, but for some extraordinary reason, probably as a result of the general confusion, a group of workers (not employed by him) intervened and insisted upon his release. This final warning galvanized Simon into leaving Petrograd. At last giving up the collapsing Jasny empire, he struck out for the Ukraine, stopping first in Kiev. Discovering that he was being pursued by authorities who wished to rectify their error of permitting the capitalist to escape, Simon was forced to keep moving. He knew he should go abroad while it was still possible to do so, but he could not bring himself to leave his homeland. Bewildered, he wandered about, according to his own description, "kak zayats" (like a rabbit), down to Odessa, then to the Crimea, then back north, finally losing himself in Moscow, where he assumed correctly that for a while at least he could maintain anonymity among the masses.

Naum, like his father, saw no future in Petrograd after the takeover, so he quickly left.

I had moved to Petrograd in mid 1916 because of my work in the Groman bureau, but after the Bolsheviks took power there was no point in remaining there. So we returned to Kharkov in the Ukraine, where the mill with which I was associated was located and where we still had an apartment.

Kharkov was the capital of the Ukraine then. Political regimes changed every few months. It so happened that the bank of the river where our mill was located, half a block from my apartment (but it was not a water mill), was a favorite place for the shooting by each new regime of the adepts of the departed or departing regime. Conditions were understandably unsuitable for the type of literary work I wanted to do, but I stuck to it. I contributed on rare occasions to a daily (the Menshevik paper for the Ukraine) and regularly to an economic weekly published by the Union of Trade Cooperatives of the Ukraine. I published two pamphlets, one of them under the absurd title *Can the Ukraine Be Economically Independent?** (Of course it could, only the prospects for the independent state were not as rosy as some Ukrainians visualized.) I was also working on a large book, of which I do not now remember the title, but it certainly was devoted to grain.

Life in the meantime was becoming more and more difficult. When the regime was Bolshevik, I was capitalist, and capitalists were losing their lives easily at that time; when General Denikin or Wrangel held the whip,[3] I was a Jew, and Jews on frequent occasions were thrown out of railway windows. I had a few escapes from the regimes of both types, the recollection of which gives me considerable pleasure. I do not tell about them here because at least some of them may sound unbelievable. It was just great luck that my wife, the two girls,[4] and I came through all this unscratched. Under more favorable conditions, it is true, Mulya, my wife, might have reached a greater age than fifty years; she was the weakest of us four.

---

* The pamphlet was a criticism of a pamphlet signed with the initials A. B. (if I remember correctly). The author actually was Nikolai Popov, a prominent Menshevik with a penchant for pseudonyms, who shortly afterwards turned Bolshevik without frankly announcing this to his party friends and must therefore be considered a traitor. He was later editor of *Pravda* for many years. I feel happy to have discovered early that something was wrong with the man. The joy is lessened though by the fact that I had not been sufficiently aggressive. Another detail in connection with the pamphlet on Ukrainian independence was that the owner of the shop which printed it said of me, "This is the author who composes in print?" How right he was. I never again changed so much during the printing process, but all my long life I have had difficulties with publishers owing to excessive changes in proof. On two occasions I paid sizeable amounts. I did it cheerfully.

One of the "escapes" Jasny mentions came about as a result of the fact that as a very active member of the Citizens' Guard, he kept in his apartment a cache of guns and ammunition. The apartment, located on the top floor of a building near the flour mill, came under suspicion by the People's Militia, who employed the technique of night raids in their search for hidden ammunition. Fortunately, Jasny was warned in time, and shortly before the militia arrived, he and his family carried the guns and cartridge boxes downstairs to the street, leaning them in plain sight against the building. In due course, the People's Militia arrived, searched the apartment, and found nothing. Furthermore, in the dark they failed to notice the incriminating evidence leaning against the building in the street below. Another timely warning of impending arrest and probable execution sent Naum into hiding in the country for several months, during which time even his family did not know his whereabouts. They, too, were kept safe during this ordeal by acquaintances who took them into their home. It is small wonder that these terrifying experiences left their imprint on the child Natascha in the form of a deep and lasting hatred for and fear of guns.

With anti-Semitism at a peak in the Ukraine, Jews had reason to fear for their lives. Indeed, the period from 1919 until 1922 was punctuated with Jewish massacres.[5] Fortunately, having married a gentile, Jasny was not always taken for a Jew, a situation he was loath to take advantage of. However, sometimes when his family's welfare was involved, he did so in spite of his reluctance. Once, for example, when he and Natascha were waiting in line to buy milk, an old Jewish lady stood in front of them. When it came her turn, the babushka who ladled out the milk announced, "Oh, I'm very sorry, but I don't have any more milk."

The old lady, disappointed, turned away, and Naum, next in line, queried the babushka, "You don't have any more milk?"

"Oh, yes," she replied, "you can have some milk."

"But why," he asked, "didn't you give any to the old lady?"

"I don't sell milk to Jews,' she snorted. Natascha saw the pain in her father's face as he repressed his pride and said nothing.

With spiraling inflation, money was becoming increasingly short, and food was becoming more and more difficult to obtain. Naum acquired a job teaching at the university, and his writing brought in a few rubles. Although Mariya was again pregnant, she, too, added a small amount to the family treasury by substituting for a dentist who was gone from Kharkov for a few months.

In spite of the fact that Mariya had attended medical school, she did not minister as the family doctor. That position was held undisputed by Naum, and he prescribed one standard remedy, whatever the ailment, a good stiff dose of castor oil. Furthermore, he had a unique method of administering it. The process became almost a ritual for Natascha, who was his prize patient. First Naum cut a lemon in half, then he rubbed Natascha's lips with it. Next came the dreaded spoonful, and finally, a reward for cooperation, the half lemon to suck on. Children all over the neighborhood were dispatched by their parents to observe "that child who takes castor oil best," hopefully to profit from her example.

On April 8, 1918, a second girl was born to the Jasnys. They named her Tatyana (Tanya). Soon after the baby's birth, Mariya developed uremia and very nearly died. In the late fall of 1918, when she had partially recovered, the doctor advised that she go south to the coast to recuperate. Mariya, Natascha, Tanya, and their fifteen-year-old country maid took the train to Anapa (in Krasnodarski Krai) on the Black Sea, where they lodged in a tiny peasant hut. It was cramped, uncomfortable, and far below the standard to which they were accustomed. The beds were merely two benches. Mariya slept on one, and the two children on the other. The maid slept in the kitchen. Contrary to expectations, Mariya's health did not improve. In fact, she contracted typhoid fever, and to make matters worse, the baby came down with dysentery. Nine-year-old Natascha and the little maid had their hands full as they watched Mariya burn with fever and the baby grow weaker every day. The little one could keep nothing on her stomach but water, and indeed there was little else to give her. When the doctor indicated that there was no hope for Tanya, Natascha wrote to her father, begging him to come quickly.

When Mariya and the children had left Kharkov, it had not yet been taken by the Bolsheviks, but by the time Natascha's letter reached her father (in late December or early January), the city was under seige and about to fall to the Reds.[6] Taking with him only a suitcase, Naum shoved his way onto the vestibule of the last train traveling south out of Kharkov. The cars were packed with people trying to avoid Bolshevik rule. Unable to squeeze inside the car, Naum settled himself on his suitcase for the long, bleak ride. After several hours of intense cold, someone noticed the huddled figure on the suit-

case, and realizing that he was probably freezing to death, dragged
Naum into the lavatory, set him on the toilet seat, and poured vodka
down his throat, gradually reviving him.

Arriving in Anapa, Jasny found to his dismay that although
Mariya was improving, she had grown appallingly thin and had lost
nearly all of her hair from the fever. Not that much, however, could
be said for little Tanya, for she was indeed dying. There was no milk
available, and her wasted body rejected all solids. One food was
relatively plentiful—potatoes. Painstakingly Naum worked with the
potatoes, slicing them very thin, spreading them in the sun to dry,
and finally, scraping the starch from them, he added it to water, a
little at a time, and offered it to the baby. She took it, and was able
to keep it down. Gradually, under her father's diligent nursing, she
began to gain strength, and before long, Naum's patience was rewarded. Tanya would live.

After several months, with Tanya recovered and Mariya showing
improvement, Naum and his family traveled east to Kislovodsk, the
resort town in the North Caucasus where the elder Jasnys had sought
refuge before them.

GEORGIA

Early in 1920 my family and I were cut off from Kharkov in Kislovodsk, in the North Caucasus, by the Bolshevik occupation of
Kharkov. With anti-Semitism under the Generals Denikin and then
Wrangel in full swing, and other unpleasantnesses in abundance, staying in Kislovodsk did not make sense, so I accepted an invitation of
Seid Devdariani, vice-president of the Georgian Social-Democratic
party to come to Tiflis (now Tbilisi) to help them out. (Under
Social-Democratic leadership, Georgia was a politically independent
but economically rather helpless republic at that time.) It was quite
a task to get there, though (this trip to Tiflis should be included in
the dangerous escapes mentioned above).

In Tiflis I had a job in the Ministry of Food, and operated
(temporarily) as a flour-mill technician by directing the construction
for the Mininstry of Defense of a plant for cleaning grain. (Having to
pay rent in kind, the tenants of State land delivered the wheat in a
horrible state; less than 50% was wheat, and although part of the rest
was made up by barley, there was also a great proportion of foreign

matter which included many poisonous kernels.* Georgia was technically even more backward than Russia proper, and in flour milling it was as bad as or worse than in anything else.) I also contributed to *Borba*, the Russian-language daily of the Social-Democratic party in Georgia (they had a daily also in Georgian).

As I mentioned, the first meeting of the Soviet of Workers' and Soldiers' Deputies in Petrograd was opened by Chkheidze, a Georgian. Irakli Tseretelli, a Georgian, was the most important member of the Kerenski government. Seid Devdariani, mentioned above, another Georgian, was the leading Menshevik in Kharkov. There were more Georgians prominently active in the Menshevik party of Russia. It was wise of course on the part of the Georgian Social-Democratic party to try to learn from the errors of the Menshevik party in Russia. But, if the Menshevik party in Russia was to be made morally responsible for the Bolshevik Revolution, as many Georgian Social-Democrats believed, its Georgian members were as guilty as everybody else.

After the Bolshevik Revolution the few Mensheviks in Tiflis who were not Georgians were not really treated as comrades. The most outspoken case in this respect was when the leaders of the Second International, among them Vandervelde, de Brucker, and Karl Kautzky separately, visited Tiflis. Nobody of the few non-Georgian Mensheviks, not even Sonya Zaretskaya, a prominent member of the Menshevik party, was invited (or permitted; I do not know whether any attempts from their side were made) to see the foreign guests.

Life in Tiflis was bearable at first, but in a year, prices increased about tenfold, while salaries were raised only by 50%. Near the end, one's salary had to be spent within hours of receiving it, for by the next day its exchange value in food was less. I used to cash my honorarium in *Borba* at lunch time. An article of a type which could not be written in a few hours brought so little that no more could be bought for it than a small piece of corn bread (we were buying white bread only for the baby) and two good apples—a lunch for effective slimming.

Then in March, 1921, if I remember correctly, the Bolshevik

---

* In Gori and the vicinity, practically everybody had spoiled black teeth. Gori happens to be the birthplace of Stalin. The association of immense technical backwardness of Stalin's birthplace with a general abundance is certainly of great interest.

invasion of Georgia started (they called it liberation, of course), and it proceeded at a rapid rate. We decided to go abroad.

If our sources are correct, Jasny was somewhat confused on the date of the invasion, for David M. Lang, in his book on Georgia, reports that the Reds attacked Tbilisi on February 25.[7]

On the night before the invasion, the Jasnys, along with President Noe Zhordania and other members of his staff, boarded the last train out of Tbilisi for Kutaisi, where Zhordania hoped to set up his headquarters. Naum and his family, however, did not remain in Kutaisi but journeyed on to Batum, the coastal town where they intended to book passage on a ship bound out of the Black Sea.

Unfortunately, when they arrived in Batum, there was no ship available. Furthermore, there were no houses or apartments to be rented. With his usual resourcefulness, Naum located a one-room schoolhouse—which was not being used, since the schools were not functioning at the time—and the Jasnys, with their few possessions, moved in. The accommodations were barely adequate. There was a stove to cook on, and a table, a piano, and the piano bench to sleep on. The table was big enough for Naum, Mariya could stretch out on the bench, and Natascha and Tanya could curl up together on the piano. Considering everything, it was as comfortable as could be expected.

Mariya apparently found her lack of experience as a cook rather inconvenient, although potatoes do not require a great deal of practice to prepare. There occurred, however, one major culinary disaster. One day Naum sauntered into the little schoolroom, triumphantly displaying a chicken, their first meat in weeks. With eager anticipation, the children watched Mulya clean it and put it in a pot to boil. Hungrily they all drank in the aroma as the chicken bubbled on the fire. At last it was tender and ready to eat, but the first bite turned delight into shattering disillusionment. Mariya inadvertently had "salted" the chicken with sugar. There is no need to expound on the children's disappointment and the sensitive woman's chagrin when she realized her improvident mistake. Bravely, her family choked down the meat; but the sweet broth was too much even for their starved tastes, so Mariya threw it out.

For six weeks the Jasny family lived in the schoolhouse, waiting for a boat that would not come. The Bolsheviks contracted the circle ever tighter, and Turkey leered threateningly at Georgia's southern border. Around the middle of March the Red army entered Batum, thus posing a serious threat for Naum Jasny.[8] At this unfortunate time, Natascha contracted a severe ear infection, just before the long-hoped-for ship did indeed arrive in the Batum harbor. The doctor insisted that Natascha must not leave, but Naum had no choice. It could well be his last opportunity, as the Soviets were beginning to inspect outgoing vessels. Assured that another ship would arrive shortly, Naum reluctantly bade his family goodbye and climbed on board. Fortunately, the captain obtained permission to proceed without inspection, and Naum was safe. Natascha's ear improved rapidly, so that by the time the second ship arrived, Mariya and the girls also were ready to sail.

The accommodations were less than first-class, however, for the boat had transported to Batum a load of coal, and in their haste the crew neglected to sweep up the dust before loading the passengers.

As the boat approached Constantinople, Natascha and Tanya, wearing bright red coats made for them out of the heavy drapes from their Kharkov apartment, pressed against the rail in order to look around the harbor. Naum's boat was much slower than the one his family was on; consequently, the two ships approached the port at the same time. Recognizing the vessel just behind as the one which should be bringing his family, Jasny borrowed the captain's telescope and peered hopefully along the railing of the approaching boat. "And there," he reported to them later, "there I saw those two little red devils, and I knew you were on board."

Part II

AUSTRIA, GERMANY: MAKING A NEW LIFE

4—Vienna: An Unfulfilled Promise

A NEW LIFE

The boat took us to Trieste. There was a stop at Piraeus on the way. We visited the Acropolis, I carrying the little girl [three-year-old Tanya] on my shoulders. Perhaps it was the immense contrast between the conditions we were leaving behind and the peaceful ruins 2,500 years old, but the impression that the Acropolis made on me was the greatest of my life.

A second stop for the Jasnys was the island of Corfu, which made a stronger impression on Natascha than on Naum. Assigned to look after her little sister in the marketplace while her father shopped for oranges, the twelve year old became alarmed upon being separated from her father by the crowd. Clutching Tanya's hand, she desperately searched among the multitude for the familiar figure. At last, in the distance she spied her father, and with immense relief, ran to his side. Naum, however, completely absorbed by his immediate task, remained oblivious of the fact that his children were lost, until Natascha informed him.

Upon arriving in Trieste, the Jasnys directed their steps towards Vienna, where Naum's father and mother were already well established. Judging from the nostalgia reflected in his writing at this point, we conclude that Naum had fond recollections of his university days in Vienna and that he cherished the hope that in this gentle city lay his future. Unfortunately, Vienna was to fulfill little of its promise to him during the two years in which he lived there.

The post-World War I division of the Austro-Hungarian Empire left what was designated the Republic of Austria in an impossible situation. Separated from the rest of what had been a viable empire, Austria was reduced to some eight million inhabitants and was saddled with thirty years of reparations.[1] One-fourth of that population resided in Vienna itself, which had been a great industrial city but whose markets were now walled in by high tariffs imposed by the surrounding countries. The resulting deterioration of the city was accelerating in 1921, with inflation, severe food shortage, and unrest being the most obvious symptoms. This was the Vienna to which Naum Jasny returned, hoping to begin a new life.

Having arrived in the city with virtually no money, Jasny accepted temporarily a clerk's position in his father's bank, hoping soon to find a pursuit more to his liking. Housing was exorbitantly expensive within the city; therefore, after they had stayed for a few days in his parents' apartment, Naum rented comfortable quarters for his family in Linz, while he found for himself a tiny room in Vienna so that he could be near his work. On occasional overnight visits, his family crowded in with him, all four attempting to sleep on the mattressless bed, the two children on one side, and Naum and Mariya on the other.

At the end of this section of his memoirs, Jasny refers to Vienna as a "grave," probably because he found little opportunity for research and publication there. However, the two years were not a total loss to his career, for he did manage to publish several articles, one of which he includes in his memoirs as his "favorite article."

In addition to the article described as "my favorite," I published in a Russian daily in New York one or two others. I also published (in German) in *Kampf*, the publication of the Austrian Social-Democratic party, a critique of Kautsky's pamphlet *Georgia*, another attempt to have the truth said, however disagreeable this might be. The essence of my criticism was: "Democracy and all that is fine, but one should not look at things through rose-colored spectacles." The article brought me together with Kautsky's sons, Benedict and Karl. Kautsky himself treated me cordially, when I paid him a visit, but this cannot be said of the remnants of the Georgian government then in Vienna. I left Georgia with a Georgian passport, but was compelled to shift to a Soviet passport. Now it is difficult to visualize the conditions then, but the fact is that I was given a passport, although I designated myself as a Menshevik.*

I lived in Vienna in 1921. Vienna was created by nature to be a place of merriment. Less than a hundred kilometers to the west the Alps start to become real mountains, majestic, frequently sinister. Still further west the mighty snow-covered Mont Blanc, Monte Rosa, and Jungfrau rise into the sky. But around Vienna there are only tiny soft hills, hills of great loveliness. These natural surroundings, as is well known, found their most refined expression in the music of Mozart and in the famous Vienna waltzes—hundreds, perhaps thousands, of waltzes, none of them boisterous like the mazurka, but soft, tender, loving.

In 1921 the landscape was of course the same, but the merriment was missing. The aftereffects of the war were very strong in many countries. For Vienna there was in addition the fact that the capital of a country with some fifty million inhabitants had suddenly lost almost all its hinterland, had become a head without a body. The usually merry Vienna was indeed grey in 1921.

My family lived in Linz, about a hundred kilometers away. I myself lived in a big house somewhere behind the Nash market. The laundry and ironing rooms of the house were located in the attic, on about the eighth floor. One had to walk up. The houseowner had put into the tiny ironing room a bed, a little table, a chair, and a portable oven for coal briquettes, and then rented it for a few kronen. The bed had no mattress on its open spring base. I remember this vividly. When winter came I was so cold in bed that I could not sleep. Heaping on everything warm did not help. With my absent-mindedness, it took me some time to realize that the cold was coming from below. Everything went fine after a blanket was put under the bed sheet.

Food was scarce. Everybody seemed to be more or less hungry. Bread was rationed, but as a foreigner I did not have a bread card. There were some particularly cheap restaurants or sections of restaurants. They were called, I believe, *Gemeinschaftsküche*. I remember one menu—soup (of the type described below) and a potato ball (*knödel*) with goulash sauce. The goulash was served on the regular

---

* There existed at that time a permission of the respective party organizations for the members to describe themselves as without party affiliations (*bezpartiiny*) but I did not know of this.

menu, but they made an extra large amount of sauce with it, so that some could go to the customers of the *Gemeinschaftsküche*.

Normally I went for dinner to a regular restaurant. It was a nice restaurant too. Menu: 1. the good Vienna water, but yellow-colored and heated with a few kernels of pearl barley or vermicelli in it; 2. the tiniest piece of meat, perhaps one ounce, a not too heaped spoonful of potatoes, and a similar amount of carrots; and 3. a roll made from real white flour, the size of a large prune, with a cherry on top.

There were items which were really cheap. I was interested in two of them: railway tickets (because of my visits to the family) and grand opera—upper gallery, standing. The tickets for the latter went on sale the same day about 6 P.M. On my way home from the office I had to change trams at the opera. I would run to see whether there was any chance of a ticket: there was a turnstile before the ticket window, and a mark on the adjacent wall, showing the point beyond which queuing was hopeless. If there was a real chance, I would take my place in the turnstile queue, get the ticket, buy at a delicatessen a roll (*semmel*) and something to go with it, and wait for the start.

It was impossible for me to stand for a whole evening on the diet I was getting, so I used to hire from the theater official his chair for a few hellers. One could not see the stage from it, but as the operas were mostly familiar, it was fine just to hear the singing and the music. At great moments it was possible to get up and try to find a place from which at least part of the stage was visible. After having treated myself to all these luxuries, I walked the few miles home.

New Year's Eve is traditionally a great night in Vienna. The merriest night of the year. The center of the celebration was, and probably still is, Kärtnerstrasse, leading from the incomparable Ring to St. Stephen's Kirche. The huge crowd would walk on the left side down the street, turn at the church, and return on the right side. Turning before the church or crossing the street was not permitted. There were plenty of police on hand to enforce the order.

It was raining the evening before the entrance of 1922. I left home, intending to take a tram to the center of the city. But it turned out that for some reason the trams were not running that night. So I walked. When I reached the Kärtnerstrasse, the usually boisterous and noisy street was almost absolutely empty, except for the usual lines of policemen on both sides, who were enforcing the rules on not turning and not crossing, which made sense when great crowds were moving about but had a gruesome effect when there was a fair distance from one celebrator to the next.

Having escaped into a side street, I directed my steps to the famous Café Central in the Herrengasse, frequented in earlier days by Trotsky and Bukharin. Everything in the café was as it had been yesterday and the day before: a few regular customers reading papers, writing letters, playing chess, hardly chatting, and certainly nobody celebrating.

There was nothing left to do but walk home in the rain. The walk being quite long, I thought about the content of a New Year's article (I had a small unpaid outlet) and, on reaching home, wrote it down. The title was "Not Merrily Did Vienna Usher in the New Year." Every paragraph started with this sentence. It was supposed to read like a poem in prose.

After a few hours of sleep, I went to the house of my parents and read the article to them. My good mother, of course, liked the product of her eldest son. But my father flatly refused to believe that his good-for-nothing offspring could have produced anything of the sort, particularly in so short a time.

The article appeared in a Russian newspaper, *Utro* (published in New York), on January 25, 1922, with slight editorial changes, including the title.

It may be strange that a man who hopes to have factual findings of more or less permanent value cherishes most a piece in which what is said is secondary and how it is said occupies the first place. And yet we value low what we have, however important it may be, while we value high what we do not have, however minor it may be. Perhaps there is another explanation. Research, as I understand it, is the more productive the more one succeeds in suppressing all feelings. So one is happy to have an opportunity where such suppression is not required.

VIENNA TODAY
(January 1, 1922)

It was not with gaiety that Vienna was seeing in the New Year.

Emptiness in the streets leading to the center.

In the famous Café Central, which prides itself on the table at which Peter Altenberg used to sit, a few habitués sniff at their black coffee and read the papers.

The neighboring cafés are even more abysmal.

There is something of a crowd only in St. Stephen's Square, traditionally the center for seeing the New Year in. But even here they are not celebrating. The crowd consists almost entirely of people who are hanging about, interested in seeing the large force of policemen. A strange sight, indeed, these hundreds of guards standing close in line to keep strict order amongst a public which has no disorder in it. There must, surely, be some grounds of concern for the safety of the shop windows. Maybe the fright comes from December 1st.[2]

A crow, once frightened, is afraid of a bush.

On Kärtnerstrasse, near the Opera House, there are not many people. The principal cafés here are almost empty. Some of them are closed. Further on, again just occasional individuals hurrying home.

No joy, not even anything that can be called liveliness. No fine clothes; no merry jokes. In poverty-stricken Vienna there is no Viennese stylishness; none of the famous Viennese humor. Everywhere, depressed, worried, or indifferent people.

There is nothing to gladden the Viennese. Nothing to remember the old year for, and nothing to expect of the new.

The trade revival caused by the fall in the value of the krone is already subsiding. The old cheap goods are sold out. The new ones are frighteningly dear. Austrian industry, in disorder, without resources, cannot produce cheaply. Emptiness in the shops, once again. The foreigners have poured in, like distant relatives come to divide up an estate. The Viennese, of course, stays where he is. There is nowhere for him to go. He stays with the empty shelves, with the unbearably rising cost of living, with the milliard of paper money printed every day, with the prospect of a 200–300 milliard budget deficit, with all his other sorrows.

And now, as if for Christmas and the New Year, the government has whipped him with financial scorpions. In a hopeless effort to master what cannot be mastered, the government passed through Parliament in a few days a number of very severe financial laws. And the minister of finance has added, for his part, no small number of his own orders.

Which Viennese doesn't have at the present time—whether for speculation or for a rainy day—eighteen dollars?

They were worth on December 22 over 100,000 kronen
—the maximum sum up to which, according to the new law,
foreign currency need not be declared. He worried all Christmas week: to declare or not to declare? The law, it is true,
requires only declaration and denies absolutely any intention
to confiscate. But the Viennese doesn't trust it. He knows
the State has its back to the wall and, not without cause, is
afraid that, on the Russian example, first they will register
and then confiscate.

The period allowed for declaration elapsed on 31 December. And not a few Viennese who, after much wavering,
did not declare their foreign currency, passed New Year's Eve
in apprehension. A heavy sword of Damocles hangs over
them: the law threatens up to ten years' imprisonment for
failure to declare.

Perhaps it is only the banker, as a successful speculator,
who can now forget even for a moment about January eighth
—that fatal date which, in accordance with another new law,
begins the abolition of the long-established practice of state
food subsidies. Until quite recently the state supplied a loaf
(1,320 grammes) for 12.80 kronen, which did not cover even
the cost of baking. The price has just gone up to 72, and on
January eighth the same loaf will cost over 300. In March,
and perhaps sooner, the price will be higher still. And then,
a month or so later, bread will be sold at cost, however high.
As for flour, fats, and other foods, the price pegging at the
cost of the State is to cease entirely on that January eighth.

What will be the consequences of this new law? Will
it succeed in reducing by some tens of millions a deficit of
200–300 milliards, or will the new rise in the cost of living
caused by this measure still further devaluate the krone, increase the state's expenditures, and end up by making the
deficit larger? Who can answer this question with any confidence? In any case, not the Allied advisers at whose demand this step was taken. The Viennese expects the worst.
Despondently counting the new blue notes, he sees with
dismay that they are not enough.

These two laws are far from the whole picture of the
new taxation pressure on the unhappy Viennese. The law
on advance payment of personal tax, the law on increased
payment of property tax, the law against flight of capital.
And then orders by the minister. There is plenty to be
miserable about.

True, the government has given the Viennese a New Year's present. At last, after nearly a year of coming and going, it has become possible to arrange a loan. But on what conditions? As security for the loan, Vienna must give her beauty, her pride. Her art galleries.

It has been possible to keep back from the pawnshop only the Gobelin tapestries and some other items. Like the wretch who has just pawned the last child's coat and, counting the coppers, assures himself: "I won't spend this on drink. This money will put me straight and I'll redeem the coat," the Viennese tries to assure himself that he will not eat up the money received on the security of the art treasures, he will set up a bank, stabilize the currency, and live well again. But he knows perfectly well that on the two or three million English pounds that, at best, he will be able to get, no bank can be established. The amount will scarcely suffice to get through the next two or three months. And then—again begging, again humiliations.

Happily, not all of Vienna has yielded its spirit to the influence of all this currency, financial, and other mess. There are plenty who, refusing to lose their heads, stoically endure all the misfortunes with a firm confidence in the fate of their beloved Vienna and look to the future. They are sure that Vienna has not died, that it will have a new life, will once again be the beautiful, lively, merry Vienna, even without Gobelin tapestries or with new ones. And they are right. It was not without reason that the Viennese, whether industrialist, merchant, banker, doctor, scholar, or artist, formerly served a population of fifty million. The Viennese industrialist is more competent; the Viennese merchant and banker more resourceful; the Viennese scholar more learned; the Viennese doctor better able to cure; the Viennese artist a finer performer than those of the other peoples inhabiting former Austro-Hungary. They are all consistently more cultured than their neighbors. And therein lies their strength. Culture will take what is due to it. Culture conquers.

But now it is a hard, a very hard life for that beauty, Vienna.

It was not with gaiety that she saw in the year 1922.

A. NAUMOV

Vienna, 1 January 1922

ADJUSTMENT

In the summer of 1922 the Jasnys found their separation except on weekends too great a burden, and Naum located a primitive little farm cottage in Bad Vöslau, a suburb of Vienna. There, at least, they could all live together. The inconveniences were considerable, however, for they had only an outdoor privy and were obliged to pump their water from a well in the courtyard.

Mariya, apparently, was not content in this foreign land. She did not speak German, her health was still poor, she tired easily, and she missed her homeland desperately. But she did not complain to her husband, who had difficulties of his own, not the least of which must have been the frustration over his work and the lack of adequate income.

Meanwhile, Natascha, by then thirteen, was struggling with a problem at school. The institution which she attended was Catholic, and it imposed considerable religious instruction on the pupils. Already feeling intrusive because she had been reared as a Protestant, the child found to her dismay that her teacher was extraordinarily anti-Semitic. He seemed to be obsessed with his hatred, to the extent that virtually all his instruction consisted of propaganda attacking the Jews. Natascha, sitting in the front of the room, dreaded the consequences of his ever learning that her father was a Jew. One day, unfortunately, the instructor determined to ask each child what the religion of his parents was. Starting at the back of the room, he insisted that every youngster in turn recite, "My mother is ——; my father is ——." Natascha listened with growing horror as the exercise progressed. At last it was her turn. Terrified, she could not find her voice to speak.

"What is your mother?" the teacher prompted.

"My mother is a Protestant," she replied.

"Well, then," he assumed impatiently, "your father is a Protestant too."

Natascha did not correct him, and he turned to other matters.

Unfortunately, there was little relief for the sensitive child, for she recognized her silence as a lie. It was the first of her life, and the impact of the deed was devastating. Natascha developed a debilitating earache, which kept her from going to school, and all the talents of the Viennese doctors could not relieve it; but then, they had no reason to suspect its psychosomatic nature. Eventually the earache went away, but the memory and guilt of that horrible experience were to haunt Natascha for years.

Meanwhile Naum's brother Simon was finding life in the Soviet Union increasingly threatening. After numerous arrests and a trial by the High Tribunal, which was prosecuted by the notorious N. Krylenko, Simon gratefully accepted a friend's offer to arrange for a passport, and in 1923 he left the Soviet Union for Berlin.

By this time Naum Jasny was beginning to recognize that Vienna's promise for him was not to be honored. He must move on if he was to further his career in research.

While life after I left Petrograd in December, 1917, was difficult and dangerous and in any case nothing to be happy about, Vienna, the beautiful Vienna with its Ring, quais, and parks, was no better for me than a grave. I owe gratitude to my brother Simon for urging me to leave it, come what may.

5—*Germany: A Good Place to Work*

BERLIN

The decision to move from Vienna to Berlin proved to be a very happy one, although I had to leave the family in a town near Vienna to which I had moved them from Linz the previous summer. Transportation by railway cost little more than pennies, but even these pennies were lacking. Arriving in Berlin with an empty bag and five dollars, I rented the cheapest room possible, indeed one without electric light (old-fashioned gas). But in a few days I found suitable work in the journal of the Ukrainian Commissariat of Foreign Trade, published in my home town of Kharkov in the Ukraine. The arrangements were simple. I was to deliver the MSS to their representative in Berlin (it happened to be Teitelbaum, one of the accused in the Menshevik trial in 1931), and he was to pay me one dollar per typed page. I remember having written something like sixty pages or more in one week. Even before having cashed the fortune due to me, I cabled my wife to sell the few pieces of furniture we possessed and come to Berlin. Full of joy, I even went part of the way to meet them.

The flexibility of childhood enabled Natascha and Tanya soon to accept Germany as home, although the former was torn between wanting to identify with their foster country and not wishing to hurt her mother, who despised it.

Soon after their arrival, Michael Jasny, who at the age of seventy was entertaining ideas of developing a business, undertook a trip to Berlin, paying them a visit. Natascha, who greatly admired her grandfather, met him at the station, wearing her best white dress for the occasion. Proudly she steered the debonair gentleman, complete with spats, from the station towards a Konditorei, where he had promised her a treat. Stealing excited glances at him as they strolled along together, the fourteen-year-old girl failed to notice a lamppost in her path and blundered into it, raising a telltale lump on her forehead.

Michael's visit to Berlin had as its purpose the inauguration of an ambitious new idea, a food automat, the first to be built in Berlin. Indeed, shortly, that innovative gentleman established his residence in Berlin and opened an automat near the Bahnhof. Specializing in fancy sandwiches, the automat featured a restaurant at the back for those who wanted a complete dinner instead of just a snack. As would be expected, it was an immediate success, and Michael, considering the possibility of extending his operation to Paris, journeyed there to investigate the potential. Shortly before his departure, he asked his granddaughter Natascha what she would like for him to bring her from the famous city. Natascha, having recently developed an interest in art, asked for a catalog from the Louvre. Grandfather seemed puzzled by her request, but happily complied and brought her a catalog—from the Louvre Department Store. Natascha was dumbfounded, but she dutifully thanked her business-minded grandfather.

Sometime in 1923 the Jasnys were honored by the first of three visits by Naum's distinguished colleague from the Soviet Union, V. G. Groman. (Naum saw him also in 1925 and 1927.) Tanya, who was only five years old at the time, remembers him as a big, impressive man who called her Tanyichka and informed her, "If you were a little bit older and I were a little bit younger, I would ask you to wait for me."

The work for the Ukrainian Commissariat of Foreign Trade was only the beginning. Soon other and better opportunities presented themselves. While the honorariums were not high in dollars, the dollars had an immense purchasing power in German marks, until the mark was stabilized in October of the same year.

The opportunities and conditions of work for non-Communists in publications of the U.S.S.R. in the 1920s should in no case be confused with those later under Stalin. My negative attitude toward the Bolsheviks was well known, but nobody cared. I was the only man believed to be familiar with the world grain markets; there was interest in this problem in the U.S.S.R., and that settled the issue. I was publishing extensively in 1923-1925 in the U.S.S.R. itself and in the publications of the U.S.S.R. agencies in Germany. In 1923 or 1924 the well-known Eugene Varga[1] gave me an order for a long paper on the prewar grain exports of Russia. In the same period the Trade Representation of the U.S.S.R. in Germany was publishing an economic weekly as well as symposiums issued at frequent intervals (but without definite dates). The editor was the brilliant writer Nikolai Nikolayevich Sukhanov. Although he was a Communist or near Communist at that time (an unstable man, he finished as one of the accused in the Menshevik trial of 1931), it was a real pleasure to work for him. On one occasion he told me, "You, Jasny, you write about such boring stuff. At least take your reader by the throat, shake him up, and tell him that he will be at a great loss if he neglects your writings." I still remember this admonition after almost forty years, and I try, when writing, to think not only of what to write, but also how to write, making my material as readable as possible. I would not start on an article unless I saw an attractive title for it.

The conditions of publishing in the U.S.S.R. for non-Communists continued to be favorable until late in 1928. But to support a family of four on the income from this publishing became increasingly difficult after the German mark was stabilized.

HAMBURG

Early in 1925 I was compelled to take a job as an expert in the world grain trade with the grain branch of the Trade Representation of the U.S.S.R. in Germany. The branch was soon moved to Hamburg, and this removal disrupted my connections with literary channels.

The two years in the office of the Trade Representation were nothing pleasant to think about. I remember a girl coming into the office I worked in and declaring: "How long will you counter-revolutionaries still be suffered here?" Fate wanted it that she was transferred into my office as an assistant of a Communist who shared the office with me. After observing his work and mine, she easily realized that there was a good reason for keeping counterrevolutionaries like me on the staff of the branch. Not all accidents ended so well, however.

If I exclude the little more than two years in which I held the job with the Trade Representation of the U.S.S.R. in Germany, I can class the period from my arrival in Berlin early in 1923 to my reporting for a job with the Institut für Konjunkturforschung [Institute for Business Cycle Research] on August 1, 1929, i.e., of little more than six years, as, if not happy, in any case good, ones. I had independent work, although not all of it was to my liking. We were fed and clothed. The housing conditions were terrible, it is true. We lived for a year, probably in 1923-1924, in a former institution for criminal women in a suburb of Berlin. The former domitories had been converted into private apartments. Ours consisted of four cells, of which one was made into a kitchen. The cell I used as a study room had one wall completely wet. I escaped damage by sleeping in Mulya's room. The worst part of it was that from time to time there were sewage floods, the sewage rising to several inches deep on the floor of the hall along our cells. This horrible housing accommodation was the worst we had in Germany. But decent accommodations—very modest indeed, but clean, without smells, and, moreover, our own, not the worst part of an apartment subrented from somebody—we had only in the last two or three years of the ten we lived in that country. But nobody in the family complained about the poor housing or anything else, so we made do.

On March 14, 1927, I was informed by my employer, the Trade Representation of the U.S.S.R. in Germany, Hamburg branch, that I was to be dropped, effective March 15. It was ignored that by German law, to which the organization was committed, at the date stated my dismissal could not be effective before July first at the earliest. They correctly decided that anybody with relatives in the Soviet Union would not dare to appeal to a German court.

Although I was provided with literary work for a time, the prospects seemed poor. The available work was to end, and nothing was in sight for later. Mulya, my wife, was the only one who did not say the situation was desperate; I am extremely grateful to her for this. The prospects only seemed poor, it is true. That dismissal was to turn out the beginning of a really free life for me, and of my ultimate liberation from Soviet power. Even the prospects which I feared were not in the near future. The second edition of the *Encyclopedia of Soviet Export* was in preparation. I was the editor of and chief contributor to its voluminous section on grain. Amazing as it may seem, I published in 1928–1929 a whole book (in installments) from

Hamburg right in Moscow, in the Soviet monthly journal *Socialist Economy*. There was also other literary income.

Of the more important publications of the period after our settling down in Hamburg the following seem to be worthy of mention:

1. An essay on "Russian Wheat" in *Landwirtschaftliche Jahrbücher* [Agricultural economics yearbook]. It was favorably reviewed in a Russian journal by Flyaksberger, then the greatest expert on wheat in the world. I was pleased when the future proved me right in the only point Flyaksberger criticized (I believed white spring wheat, even hard white spring wheat, to be unsuitable for Russia's semiarid regions, while the introduction of this wheat in those areas was his favorite idea).

2. *Grain Elevators in North America and Russia*, a pamphlet published in 1925 in Moscow by Tsentrosoyuz, a cooperative organization. The pamphlet tried to show that the basic principle on which the Russian elevator system was based, both in the tsarist time and later under the Soviets (but still under the former leadership) was not workable. This contention was supported by the experience of North America. One man certainly read my pamphlet. This man was the head of the Soviet elevator system. Soon thereafter he published a piece, of course not even whispering my name, in which the existing basic principle of elevator construction was abandoned and the one suggested by me was put into operation.

3. "Die Konkurrenzfähigkeit der wichtigsten Überseeländer auf dem Weizenweltmarkt" [Competitiveness among the major nations on the world wheat market], a quite detailed analysis of production costs (including transport to London) of wheat in overseas countries (Canada, the United States, Argentina, Australia), in *Berichte über die Landwirtschaft* [Report on agricultural economy], 1928. If any of my studies was instrumental in my subsequent good fortunes in Germany, it was this analysis. In any case it played a substantial role in them.

Good prospects or bad, I continued to work hard after discontinuation of the job. The daily schedule was such: getting up at about 8 A.M., working until noon, lunch, walking to the reading room of the Hamburgisches Welt-Wirtschafts-Archiv to work there for a couple of hours on materials which could not be taken home. Dinner at about 3–3:30 P.M., short nap. Working until about 11 without interruption (Mulya would bring my evening tea to my desk). Sundays the same, except that the reading room was closed and that

Tanya, my little girl, expected to be taken to the ball game (soccer, of course) in the afternoon. Work as usual after return from the ball game.

One day a young man sitting next to me in the reading room introduced himself by saying: "I sit next to you every day, but you do not notice. I see the type of work you are doing. Here in the building is the editorial board of an economic weekly (*Wirtschafts-dienst* [Economic information service]), to which I contribute. They are very interested in your work, from what I told them, and asked you to be so kind as to drop in." So started an association which grew rapidly. In a short time I was contributing each month one of the leading articles, a review of the Soviet economy, and a review of the world grain markets.

My leading articles were also devoted to the world grain markets, but they were of less current character. While each of them had its own subject, I wrote them with an eye to combining them into a book. It soon turned out quite a good idea.

For nearly five years the Jasny family resided in Hamburg, during which time Natascha matured into a young lady and began to study mathematics at the university. Settling comfortably into the student life of Hamburg, Natascha let her Russian identity slip gradually away. Tanya, too, was quite content. Only Mariya remained unset-tled, probably partly because she still had not learned to speak the language, but largely because of her health, which had not been nor-mal since her bout with typhoid, was deteriorating steadily. She tired more easily and seemed to be growing weaker, but she did not com-plain to Naum.

One of Natascha's principal teachers at the university was a talented young mathematician with a vibrant personality, Emil Artin. He and Natascha soon developed a friendship which flourished under Naum's approval and culminated in their marriage a few days after Natascha's twentieth birthday. Shortly after Natascha's wedding, the Jasny family returned to Berlin, leaving their older daughter in Ham-burg with a heavy heart.

RETURN TO BERLIN

Around mid 1929 I got a letter from a friend in Berlin, suggesting that I come there, because two German institutes wanted to employ me on a permanent basis. One of the institutes was the famous Institut für Konjunkturforschung [IKF]. The other was the Reichsforschungstelle für Landwirtschaftliche Marktforschung [National Department of Research for Agriculture Marketing], directed by Dr. Fritz Baade, the Reich-Getreide-Kommissar.

I talked first to Baade. I do not know what impression I made on him, but I was not enthusiastic. It was fortunate that we did not reach an understanding, because the rye problem, discussed below, would have inexorably separated us soon thereafter.

I was received really well, almost triumphantly, when I presented myself in the IKF. Dr. Arthur Hanau, their agricultural man, was familiar with every line I had published in German, and there was little to be said. Hanau was enthusiastic for me to take over part of the heavy load which he had to carry. In no time I got an invitation in writing, offering me more money than I hoped for. An obstacle turned up in that the job offered was that of a scientific helper (*wissenschaftlicher Hilfsarbeiter*). But I let myself be persuaded that it was only a formality and that all their scientific workers had this title. As it turned out, it was far from being just a formality.

I reported for the job on August 1, 1929. So far as finances are concerned, the job certainly was timely. After about a year on the staff of IKF we succeeded in getting a small apartment of our own, although the little furniture we needed had to be bought on installment payments (the only time I ever used this arrangement). Certainly no savings were left from the work done for the Soviets.

A good room with two windows and all needed paraphernalia was waiting for me in the institute, and, more important, so were two statistical assistants. There were also many other pleasing things, but also some unpleasant ones. Let me get these off my chest first.

The institute was closely connected with the State Statistical Office. The president of the office was our director, we had our offices in the building of the office, etc. The Central Statistical Office was operated in a military or bureaucratic manner of such strictness as hardly existed in Russian government offices in tsarist times. A *Herr Oberregierungsrat* (chief counselor to the government) would not enter the room of a *Herr Regierungsrat* (counselor to the government) but would let him come to his room, and so on.

The IKF was operated largely in the same way. Three high officials of the State Statistical Office, under the strict leadership of the director [Ernst Wagemann] shared the direction of the institute, being in charge of research, publications, and personnel respectively. The real analysts, while well paid, were not juniors *inter pares* but something lower than this. When, for example, the member of the triumvirate who was in charge of research went on vacation, his job would be completely inactive, although it would have been in the interests of the work if the most prominent among the scientific helpers, say Dr. Otto Donner (now a director of the International Bank for Reconstruction and Development and professor at Georgetown University in Washington, D.C.) had been appointed to fill in the job until the return of the chief. The real assisting personnel had even a much lower standing than that of the scientific helpers. This personnel had even a different timetable, reporting for work and leaving one and a quarter to one and a half hours before the privileged ones. It was particularly galling that the statistical assistants were not supposed to sit in the presence of their respective chiefs. Nobody took all these arrangements so hard as I did, but, after all, nobody had left his own country with wife and children to see the elementary principles of democratic behavior stamped underfoot. Stubbornness is a protective weapon in the life which fell to my lot. My dissatisfaction with those arrangements was so great that it was a major reason among those that induced me to leave the institute soon, although otherwise I was extremely satisfied.

Dr. George (Jura) Garvy (the son of Jasny's good friend Peter Garvy), who worked as Jasny's assistant from 1930 to 1932, tells us that Ernst Wagemann, director of the State Statistical Office and the research institute as well, was a militaristic Prussian who stressed rank, discipline, and order, all three of which Jasny detested and denigrated. One is hardly surprised to learn that the two men did not always get on well together. One story about their relationship provides insight into the personalities of both.

Since the institute was located in a converted hotel, Wagemann's office was equipped with a private toilet. Jasny asked for and was granted permission to use it, a fact which led to an awkward situation. In fulfilling his assignment to keep abreast of the grain market, Jasny requested an English-language newspaper from Argentina called the Times of the River Plate, which carried detailed grain statistics for that country. He was informed that a budgetary appropriation would be requested and that the library could then subscribe to the paper the following year. Jasny's needs were immediate, and he naturally resented being told he must wait a year for research materials. Confronting Wagemann, Jasny insisted, on threat of resignation, that the newspaper be ordered immediately. Not wishing to lose a valuable research analyst, Wagemann broke all precedent and designated unused appropriations in order to fill Jasny's request. Some months later, the director was annoyed to find in his w.c. torn copies of the newspaper which had been the cause of so much difficulty. Just to be certain, he asked the librarian for those particular copies, and upon being told that they were checked out to Jasny, requested their return. Jasny said he didn't have them, whereupon Wagemann called him into his office and confronted him with the evidence. Disgusted with the attention paid to what he considered trivia, Jasny told Wagemann to go to hell, and then stalked out. Furthermore, he continued to insist upon special research materials, and Wagemann, in spite of his frustration, granted the requests.

We should perhaps point out here that however Jasny disagreed with Wagemann's regimentation and strictness, these very qualities may have been partially responsible for the excellent working conditions Jasny experienced at the institute.

Work in the institute was fantastically well organized. Of the two statistical assistants I had, one was the senior. Calling on the help of the junior assistant, the senior assistant prepared the tables and charts and did all the needed statistical analysis. He was expected to be familiar with the standard statistical procedures, even multiple correlation; and when in difficulty, he would turn to another statistical assistant for help. When typing was needed, the senior assistant would take it to the typists' pool, read the typing back with the typist, and hand the typing to me in a form I could be fully confident in. The assistants checked all references in MSS, did the proof reading, and so on. Absence of the statistical assistants in the last period of up to an hour and a half of each working day was of course an obstacle, but not a very large one. I had ample time for study of the material. All that I had to contribute was a few ideas. Indeed, in my book which attracted the greatest attention (Die Zukunft des Roggens, see below), there was only one idea: "Rye bread is a matter of the past."

The institute as such published quarterly reviews of the world economy as well as weekly reports. The contributions were unsigned and carefully edited to a certain style. In addition, special volumes (Sonderhefte) were published. They were not edited, and were signed by the names of the authors. The publishing was in the hands of Reimar Hobbing. MSS and proofs went on a schedule which was kept strictly. For the quarterly of the institute the schedule distinguished between the morning and afternoon of a day.

I was expected to be informed about the developments in the world grain markets, including that of Germany—a task I had been performing for years. On the basis of this I made my contribution to the quarterlies of the institute, a job hardly requiring more than a day each three months. On very rare occasions, contributions were requested for the weekly publication of the institute. Otherwise I, like all the others, was on my own.

I mentioned my articles in *Wirtschaftsdienst*, written so as to be easily combined into a book. I actually did this combining some time before arranging to join the IKF. As soon as I reported for my job with the latter, it turned out that something like this book was the very reason for my invitation to the institute's staff.

Of course, I offered the MS for publication as a *Sonderheft* of the institute, to the latter's great satisfaction. The manuscript needed little further work, and so it soon went to press and was on sale by the same Christmas, under the title *Die neuzeitliche Umstellung der überseeischen Getreideproduktion und ihr Einfluss auf den Weltmarkt* [The current restructuring of overseas grain production and its impact on the world market], *Vierteljahrshefte zur Konjunkturforschung, Sonderheft* 16 (Berlin, 1930).

The author of a *Sonderheft* was supposed to prepare an extract (these were written in a most restrained manner), which was mailed by the publisher to journals, magazines, and dailies in great numbers. In no time, dozens, if not well over a hundred, reviews appeared, and yesterday's status of an unknown came suddenly to an end.

The problem on the grain front of general interest in those years was that of rye, which had been Germany's most important grain crop by far (in 1929, 11.3 million tons of rye were produced, as against 3.8, 9.1, and 3.5 million tons of wheat, oats, and barley respectively), and a great campaign was in progress to support grain (in the first place, rye) prices at a level satisfactory for producers in less favorable conditions. Fritz Baade—a very able man, a brilliant writer and speaker (a touch of an at least moderately unbiased analyst would have made him perfect)—started it, with the support of the Social-Democratic faction of the Parliament, of which Baade was a member. The institute asked me to write a *Sonderheft* on the topic. Probably they knew

that the subject attracted general attention and just wanted to participate in the debate with a piece by a man they believed competent,
whatever position I might take.

After some hesitation, I started on the book on rye at the end
of January or early in February, 1930. I had the great luck to have
discovered a major error in the German foreign-trade statistics, for
which the State Statistical Office was responsible. As reward I asked
for and obtained three statistical clerks for a few months. With five
persons to handle the statistics, I produced in little more than three
months a volume containing fifty-seven tables, twenty-seven charts,
and a corresponding amount of text, which took me about seventy
days to write.

About half of the volume was devoted to a country-by-country
analysis of production and consumption of rye outside Germany,
starting as far back as statistics permitted (mostly 1880). The second
half of the book did the same with reference to Germany, but going
here into much greater detail, specifically regional analysis.

The statistical evidence was so persuasive that there was no need
to press the conclusions. Rye, once Europe's most widespread grain,
was being ever-more replaced by other grains. I concluded that the
production of rye, which is greatly favored in Germany by the conditions of climate and soil, would for some time retain a strong position,
but would in the long run follow the pattern set the world over. The
forecast was very cautious, containing no statements on the extent of
the anticipated decline or of its rapidity.

Die Zukunft des Roggens (The decline of rye) had a considerable and prolonged success. As if on signal, soon after the publication
of the book, per capita consumption of rye for food started an uninter-
rupted decline. It went down from 74.9 kilograms in 1929/30 to
33.4 kilograms in 1961, or by 55 per cent,* and the decline continues.

While the rye book was among my biggest successes, I myself
never thought much of it. The situation, the historical evidence, were
too obvious. Presented as cautiously as it was, with no prediction as
to timing or extent of the decline, the analysis was too simple, too
elementary. It took so little effort to produce the book.

---

* The figure for 1929/30 is that for the German Reich. The figure for
1961 is a weighted average for the Bundes-Republik and Eastern Germany.
Data were obtained from Dr. Roderic Plate, director, Institut für Landwirtschaftliche Marktforschung [Institute for Agricultural Marketing Research,
which had recently been established at the Landwirtschaftliche Hochschule
(Agricultural Economics High School) in Berlin], Völkenrade, Germany.

Another of Jasny's colleagues at the Business Research Institute, Dr. Otto Donner, recalls with pleasure his many friendly arguments with Jasny about the future of the U.S.S.R., Jasny being still convinced in those days that the Soviet regime would collapse under the weight of crop failure, famine, and deprivations of the citizens paying the price for rapid industrialization. Dr. Donner emphasizes, however, that Jasny's wishful thinking did not bias his research, either then or later.

Effective January 1, 1931, Dr. Arthur Hanau and I transferred to the Institut für Landwirtschaftliche Marktforschung, director Karl Brandt, now director of the Food Research Institute, Stanford University. One of the major reasons for the change, so far as I am concerned, was pointed out above. There were others, pro and con, which it is probably best not to discuss. Even now, after more than thirty years, I am undecided whether it was a wise move on my part. Statistical assistants were not supposed to stand up at the new place, but there were some other disagreeable things. So far as work was concerned, there was little change for me. Even my senior assistant, Mr. Paul Lubke, transferred with me. (The second assistant was a young boy in his first job, Jura [George] Garvy, who later held an important research job in Federal Reserve, New York, taught at Stanford and Columbia, travels over the whole world and generally is as successful as one can be.) There were many more publications of the Institut für Landwirtschaftliche Marktforschung itself than was the case in the IKF, to which I had to contribute. In addition to contributions to the publications of the institute in which several staff members participated, two of my studies were published as books in Schriftenreihe des Institut für Landwirtschaftliche Marktforschung: Bevölkerungsgang und Landwirtschaft and Die Standardisierung von Getreide [Publications of the Institute for Agricultural Marketing Research: Population growth and agriculture, and The standardization of grain]. In the first of the two, the then-crucial problem of growth of agricultural production vis-à-vis stable population growth was attacked. It was natural to devote considerable attention to France. My attention to the problem was drawn by the publications of Dr. O. E. Baker of the Bureau of Agricultural Economics, U.S.A.

Bevölkerungsgang und Landwirtschaft, although published in 1931, was written in 1930, when I was still at IKF. So in 1931 and 1932 a considerable amount of time was left for the topic I was most interested in at that time. This was the farm tractor.

Tractors were then a very recent introduction. The economics of their competition with animal power remained uninvestigated, not only in Germany, but also in the United States, which possessed more tractors than all the rest of the world together. The usual assumption was that the decisive factor was the direct saving on labor and that hence the differences in wages of farm labor were the most important factor in the competition between tractor and horse. However, a prominent German farm-management professor, after a prolonged stay in the U.S.A., came to the conclusion that the U.S.A. did not need tractors, because there was plenty of cheap oats. Oats were expensive in Germany, he reasoned, and therefore the farm tractor had a place there. I discussed the farm tractor in *Wirtschaftsdienst* and the *Sonderheft* 16, but felt that the problem needed a more thorough analysis. The outcome of this analysis was a book.

Der Schlepper in der Landwirtschaft [The tractor in agriculture], Berlin, Paul Parey, 1932, was certainly the most important piece of research made by me until then. It had only a fraction of the appeal of *Die Zukunft des Roggens*, but the latter was child's play to write as compared with the tractor book.

I operated with very simple ideas, or, more correctly, I succeeded in bringing the problems down to such simple ideas. The central idea was that the horse eats also when not working, while the tractor does not require fuel and lubricants when not in operation. The need for draught power tends to be shorter during the year in specialized farming, typical of countries with high wages, such as the United States, and to be longer in countries with general farming, typical of countries with low wages, such as Germany. The difference between the two types of agriculture in this respect turned out to be unexpectedly large. Hence, in the final analysis, the tractors proved to be more advantageous in countries with high wages, not so much because of the direct saving on the wages of the driver where the tractor was used, but because of the effect of the wage level on the whole setup of agriculture.

Another simple idea profitably used in my tractor book was that the horse of twenty years hence will be the same as that of today, but the tractor will probably be vastly improved. While a tractor might still have appeared unprofitable in many enterprises in the early 'thirties, its successor of the early 1940s or 1950s might well be profitable or even very profitable.

Publication of *Der Schlepper in der Landwirtschaft* came close to the end of my work and life in Germany. So far as research is concerned, it was the most fruitful period of my life. I worked on problems I was interested in; in the main, they were of my own choice. I had help of a quality far above everything I later had in the U.S.A.* In only three years and five months I published five books in addition to quite a lot of smaller items. No significant errors were committed.† The income was enough to avoid worry about money. After living in all kinds of holes for almost ten years, we were able to rent a completely clean apartment, having equipped it with our own, be it very modest, furniture.

According to Dr. George Garvy, the Marketing Institute—for which Jasny worked until 1933—operated on budgetary funds from the state of Prussia. Hence, Garvy relates, when Prince Bismarck (the son of the Iron Chancellor) was scheduled to pay the institute a visit, the impending event threw the staff into a flurry of excitement. A luncheon in Bismarck's honor was to be held in the conference room, and everyone at the institute was invited.

Jasny's lack of concern for his personal appearance was already well known and tolerated by his colleagues, but this time his shoes were in such a deplorable condition that someone tactfully urged

---

* Really good help in the U.S.A. I had almost exclusively in the Foreign Economic Administration during World War II, but nothing of my work there went into print.

† This statement is probably correct if the period covered is counted from August 1929, the day of my joining the staff of the IKF. In 1928 I committed an error which, although made under conditions that deprived the error of practically any importance, still haunts me occasionally. As mentioned, I was writing monthly reviews of the world grain markets for the *Wirtschaftsdienst*. The interest in the topic was not great, and the honorarium such that I had to write the piece in about a day. World production of wheat was unusually large in the crop year 1928–1929, and the prices in the world markets were correspondingly low. Since there was no ground to expect a repetition of the good world wheat crop in 1929–1930, I expressed in one of my reviews the expectation that prices might improve in the next crop year. They never did, because a circumstance interefered which I did not anticipate: the great agricultural depression started in 1929. The reviewers of the markets of numerous commodities for the almost numberless journals, weeklies, and dailies publishing such reviews cannot of course be expected to foresee such phenomena as a world agricultural crisis. But the fact that of all those reviews I remember only the error may be taken as a testimony that the error made a great impression on me. It seems certain that it made me reluctant, indeed unwilling, to make forecasts where there is even the smallest ounce of doubt.

him to purchase a new pair for the occasion. Too busy to be bothered, Jasny sent his senior assistant, Paul Lubke, with one of his old shoes to a nearby shoestore for a new pair in the same size, and condescended to wear them to the luncheon. Jasny, who was seated next to the guest of honor, found his new shoes too tight and promptly kicked them off under the table. After lunch, Karl Brandt, the director, escorted the prince on a tour around the institute, accompanied by Jasny, who, to the horror of his colleagues, walked along in his stocking feet.

TRAGEDY AND DEPARTURE

After the Jasnys' move back to Berlin, it had become apparent that Mariya's condition was growing worse, but the doctors could not discover the cause. In 1932, after two years, her illness was diagnosed as endocarditis, inflammation of the heart lining and valves, which had led to a generalized septicemia. There was no cure. Mariya went to the hospital, where she could be better cared for as she slowly wasted away, and Naum, month after month, sat at her bedside, keeping her company and writing. A maid came to the apartment during the day to look after Tanya, and Natascha came from Hamburg to be with her mother before she died. It was one of the most horrible experiences of Natascha's life, for at one point the doctor wanted to take an X-ray, and Mariya, who, although she was completely conscious, could no longer support herself in a sitting position, had to be held. As Natascha held the wasting figure on her lap, she suddenly realized that her mother's heart had ceased beating. In a few seconds the beat resumed. Evidently the doctor noted Natascha's reaction, for afterwards he asked her whether she had noticed anything. A few weeks later, Mariya's heart stopped once more, and this time it did not begin again. Her death was a deep tragedy for her family, who loved her greatly. "The kindest person I ever knew," Natascha says of her, "really a marvelous woman."

The last years of our stay in Germany were marred by the prolonged illness of Mulya and her ultimate passing away after twenty-four years of life together. To please her the tractor book was written in part as I sat next to her bed in the hospital. The book was dedicated to her memory. The author's copies have Mulya's picture in them. Now, thirty years after the event, it made me cry to write these few lines.

The message that on January 30, 1933, Hitler had become *Reichs-kanzler* hit me in the Riesengebirge [a mountain range between Germany and Czechoslovakia]. I returned to Berlin in a few days, and next day went to the U.S. consulate to inquire about a visa. There was no question about leaving or staying, although I had a valid contract for my job, calling for a very good salary until the end of the year. It was not that I foresaw the terrible cruelties against Jews and non-Jews or even that my contract would be replaced by some other arrangement providing a much smaller income than the salary I was drawing. (I am usually too busy thinking of my immediate work to pay attention to anything else.) It was simply that I had left my own country because I did not want to live under a dictatorship. Even less did I want to live under a foreign dictator. The same decision was arrived at independently of me by all of my Russian friends (mostly or excusively Mensheviks). The only difference was that I was the only one who headed directly for the U.S.A.

There were two reasons for my choice. At that time the U.S.A. had probably the best agricultural statistics in the world, and the research in my field, so far as I knew it, seemed to be very good (presumably, of course, I knew only the best, such as the publications of Dr. O. E. Baker of the Bureau of Agricultural Economics, the *Wheat Studies* of the Food Research Institute, and the like). This made me look up to the U.S.A. as a kind of heaven. The consideration that with so much research going on in my field, there would be a way for me to make a living, also of course played a great role.

Among Jasny's colleagues at the institute was a gifted woman economist by the name of Maria Phillipi, whom Jasny had known professionally for some time. Jasny's patient devotion to his dying wife greatly impressed Fraulein Phillipi, and after Mariya's death their friendship gradually grew into something stronger. However, the advent in 1933 of Hitler's takeover, plus Jasny's determination immediately to leave Germany, forced a premature decision. Maria Phillipi (Jasny called her Philya or Phil, never Maria) also wanted to leave Germany, but was unable to do so. Furthermore, she wished to continue her relationship with Naum. There was only one answer as far as Jasny could see. He asked Philya to marry him and go with him and Tanya to the United States. It was too soon for them both, and Philya had trouble deciding. Jasny had retained his Russian passport, which proved fortunate, as he and Tanya could enter the United

States under the Russian quota, which was not being filled. Philya, however, would have to go on a noncitizen passport and would lose her German citizenship. At the last moment Philya said yes, and they were married.

In getting a visa to the States there was the difficulty that I had a Soviet passport and the U.S.A. had no diplomatic relations with the U.S.S.R. But I wrote to Dr. Baker and the Food Research Institute, Stanford University, and as a result I got an "expert visa," or whatever the official name of it is. It was, of course, perfectly all right that in the consulate they made me swear that I was not a Communist, but it did not make a good impression on my fourteen-year-old daughter when they subjected her to the same treatment, and moreover insisted on doing it in my absence.

This incident apparently made a stronger impression on Jasny than on Tanya, for she no longer recalls it.

The Jasnys sailed for the United States in August, 1933, on the Majestic. On board ship, Tanya was befriended by a little minister, formerly an English teacher, who, wanting to help the youngster learn a little English, taught her the song "Swanee River." Tanya remembers coming into the New York harbor in the morning haze, overwhelmed by the skyscrapers of this strange new country which was closing in on her.

Part III

AMERICA: THE MOST
PRODUCTIVE YEARS

6 — The New World
and Grains of Antiquity

ARRIVAL

By the time Naum Jasny and his family had embarked for the United States, Naum's father, Michael, had accumulated considerable wealth from his Berlin restaurant-automat, and he and Rosa were living quite comfortably. However, with Hitler's ascension to power and the subsequent attacks on Jewish businessmen, Michael and his wife again decided to emigrate. Leaving their German marks—they were forbidden to remove them—they departed for Paris, intending to open a new automat and make their home in that city.

Simon Jasny, who had been divorced after coming to Berlin in 1923, had remarried. His wife, Victoria Gutman, a talented poet of Jewish-Lithuanian birth, was also a Soviet refugee. They too left Berlin in 1933, following Michael and Rosa to Paris, but then moved on to Spain, where their son Alexander (named after the second oldest Jasny brother) was born.

Naum Jasny and his family arrived in New York with little savings and fewer prospects. Undaunted, they sublet a few rooms temporarily, where they could do their own cooking. Naum set about seeking employment as a research analyst, and Tanya enrolled in high school, taking a public-speaking course to facilitate learning English. Nearly two months passed without income of any kind and with Naum and Philya alternately ill with influenza. At last, learning of a possible position with the Department of Agriculture, Naum traveled to Washington, D.C., and soon reported the welcome news that he had received an appointment with that department as a senior economist. A week later, Philya and Tanya joined him, moving into a simple, though very pleasant, two-story frame house in Chevy Chase, and Tanya continued her senior year at Western High. In spite of having to learn a new language, she would be ready the following spring to commence her college career at George Washington University.

Naum, through his years of research, had developed a small technical reading vocabulary in English. However, now, at the age of fifty, he was forced to learn to speak and write that language fluently if he was to have any future in American research. Typically, he commenced studying English in the most direct way he knew, by memorizing the dictionary. Hours of drill paid off surprisingly well, and before long Jasny was heard to comment with some satisfaction about another immigrant's accent, "He has the worst va-ca-bull'ary!" Even Jasny persistence could not completely surmount all the language difficulties.

Only one who has experienced it realizes what a deprivation it is to have to write (and an analyst is also a writer) in a language other than his mother tongue. Gallop, one of the editors of the *Encyclopedia of Soviet Exports* (a Russian publication), to which I contributed a lot, once said: "Strange, Jasny writes about such boring things, but you read it almost as a novel." Gallop was a very nice man and his statement was a great exaggeration, but it is still one of my most pleasant recollections. The Russian language is not easy. Repeated use of the same word, for example, common in German or English, is best avoided, even at a slight sacrifice in exactness. But properly handled, Russian is a delicate instrument.

Since 1928 I have had to publish in foreign languages. In view of my aversion to wearing other peoples' clothes, I have never had anything of mine translated from the Russian. Well or badly, I wrote it myself in the language in which it was to be published.

First I shifted to German. Goethe and Heine wrote a superb language, of course. But one is neither Goethe nor Heine. The German the common mortal uses and writes is to a Russian's taste stultified (they say *ich möchte gern*, although the *gern* is already in the *möchte*). There is in German also an aversion to the use of international words (such as telephone, export-import, production, etc.), for which a foreigner is unlikely to have much sympathy. This Germanizing, which became particularly pronounced under Hitler, but seems not to have abated after his downfall, extends even to cases when the international word itself has been Germanized. My German would not have passed a strict test. I was using, for example, *Einfuhr-Ausfuhr*, the Germanic equivalent of "import-export"—but, striving for variety, alternated the Germanic with the international words. I would do anything to avoid using the senseless word *Anschrift*, which replaced *Adresse*. The interests of civilization demand tightening of international contact rather than the isolation which is implied in ostracizing the use of international words. Still, the only linguistic difficulty I experienced during my active life in Germany was that once an editor asked: "Next time, please, let me have the article in German" (his objection was to the use of international words).

The real difficulties started when in 1933, at the ripe age of fifty, I had to shift to English—American English to be precise. Whatever abilities I possess do not include an ability to study languages. In the first years, my English was simply bad. The book *Research Methods on Farm Use of Tractors* suffered from the fact that a substantial part of the energy was spent not on *what* to say, but on *how* to say it. Even now, after almost thirty years, my English still needs a little editing, and I just do not have in my vocabulary the words to write otherwise than plainly. I do not feel the English language the way I feel the Russian and even the German.

Among other things, there are too many manuals. In my opinion the freedom of the word guaranteed by the Constitution of the U.S.A. is violated by them. It may be pettiness (there is nothing minor in my work for me), but I am unhappy when I want to write 1926/27 (one crop year) and I am forced to write 1926–1927, which may be read as two years. Colloquial words and slang are taboo for the common mortal until the words or phrases have been sanctioned by inclusion in the manuals. The outcome is that one does not feel at home in one's own work.

I have not had great difficulties with my publications in the English of Britain. This is partly because I started to publish regularly outside the U.S.A. after living there for more than fifteen years, but this is not the only reason. Indeed the only misunderstanding I have had—it involved my favorite editor, Mrs. Jane Degras of London—was when she had rewritten a piece of mine in such beautiful language that I looked in it like a crow in ostrich feathers (the signature would have told the reader that it was a crow after all). I would be only too happy to write in such a language myself, but, being unable to do so, I have to resign myself to a plainer form.

The joy of writing in a more colorful language, occasionally to write something in which *how* it is said is possibly more important that *what* is said, was the price I had to pay for becoming an émigré. But the sacrifice was well compensated by the gain. Only to think that in the extremely unlikely event of remaining alive, if I had not left my native country I would have *had* to write "party and government" rather than "government and party," which is taboo. In this small, seemingly indifferent, thing is the difference between freedom and slavery. With the obligatory sequence "party and government" goes the likewise obligatory lauditory treatment of all Soviet institutions and deeds, a complaisant memory which holds only the things blessed by today's party leadership, etc.

Publishing in a language other than the mother tongue is a comparatively small evil.

In spite of his language difficulties, Naum Jasny had begun to direct his research efforts towards American agriculture, producing his first article in English in December, 1935, for the American Economic Review. It was a study of the "Tractor versus Horse as a Source of Farm Power" in various countries, with emphasis on the United States and Germany. His second article, based on his German research, "Wheat Problems and Policies in Germany," appeared in Wheat Studies, published by Stanford's Food Research Institute, for whom Jasny had been a foreign correspondent before coming to the United States.

Nineteen thirty-six brought the sorrowful news that Naum's mother was dying of cancer. Michael had taken Rosa back to Berlin, where most of his money still remained, and had placed her in the most expensive hospital available. He recognized that paying the costs of her hospitalization would be the last use he would have of his German marks, since he could not take them out of the country, nor could he endure life under the Nazis. Remaining at Rosa's side until her death, he immediately set out again for Paris. Michael was seventy-eight years old, and although his Paris automat was not very successful, he still had confidence that he could rebuild his fortune.

By 1937 the only member of the Jasny family remaining in Ger-

many was Natascha. However, because she was half Jewish, her husband, Emil Artin, was soon dismissed from his position at the University of Hamburg, whereupon the Artins—by then including two children, Karin (four) and Michael (three)—sailed for the United States.

Coming into the New York harbor early in the morning, with the clouds hanging low over the city, Natascha and her family, like Tanya before them, were amazed to see the skyscrapers disappearing into the cloud cover. "Muli," cried little Karin, "Und sie kratzen wirklich!" ("Mommy, they really scrape!") It takes little imagination to visualize the joy of reunion as Naum greeted his daughter, his son-in-law, and his grandchildren at the dock. Shortly, however, they would leave for Indiana, where Artin would teach first at Notre Dame and then at Indiana University.

At the time of Natascha's arrival in the United States, Naum was finishing his first book in English, Research Methods on Farm Use of Tractors, to be published as volume 5 of Columbia University's series on the history of American agriculture. In order to acquire first-hand knowledge of agriculture in this country, Jasny applied for, and received, a grant from the Social Science Research Council. This enabled him to visit the important agricultural regions of the United States, thereby providing material for both the tractor book and a second, more ambitious study, which Jasny was already outlining, to be called Competition among Grains. Philya's first article in English appeared in the June, 1937, issue of the Political Science Quarterly: "Some Aspects of German Agricultural Settlement."

In the spring of 1938, Tanya completed her B.A. and decided to begin graduate study in social work the following fall at Simmons College in Boston. Naum accepted a temporary appointment with the Food Research Institute at Stanford University, at the same time writing his book on grains, and Philya agreed to work for agricultural economist John D. Black at Harvard University. At this point the Jasny family broke up housekeeping, Naum leaving for Palo Alto, California, and Philya and Tanya moving to Cambridge. However, after working there for only a few months, Philya was hospitalized for gynecological surgery. Tanya, under financial pressure, postponed her graduate studies for a year and found employment.

Returning from Palo Alto in the late winter, Naum Jasny took a small apartment in Washington, D.C., where he could finish work on his grain book, which Stanford University Press had agreed to publish. Tanya and Philya also returned from Cambridge, but the latter for further hospitalization and surgery. After months of severe illness, Philya suffered a mental breakdown, and Naum, determined that she should have the best care possible, placed her in a private sanitarium, where she remained until shortly before her death in March of 1941. Competition among Grains is dedicated to her.

Increasing tensions in Europe during the late 1930s convinced Naum's brother Simon and his wife Victoria that they too should emigrate. Armed with an affidavit from Naum, and sponsored by Natascha and her husband, they were granted immigrant visas to the United States in 1939. Michael, apparently disappointed by the failure of his Paris automat, concluded that the United States held more promise than war-threatened Europe for his business enterprises, and obtaining a visitor's visa, he prepared to sail with Simon and his family on the Champlain the last of August. Simon was immigrating under the Russian quota, Victoria under the Lithuanian, and Alexander under the Spanish. Unfortunately, as they were boarding the ship, the American authorities refused to honor Michael's visa, and when the ship sailed, two days before Germany invaded Poland, it left behind a disappointed but undefeated old man. Upon arriving in the United States, Simon and his family settled in New York and promptly initiated action to bring Michael over, as well.

THE CLASSICAL HISTORY PERIOD

During the period 1939 through 1940, with Philya in the hospital and Tanya having begun her graduate studies in Boston, Naum Jasny was faced with a serious financial deficit. In 1940 he reluctantly accepted an appointment to the staff of the Division of Statistical and Historical Research, Bureau of Agricultural Economics, in the Department of Agriculture, to initiate a study of the history of wheat. The following account explains in detail the approach he used, the myths he challenged, and the results he achieved in a study which proved to be a major contribution to the scholarly world. This section is especially interesting in that it demonstrates Jasny's methodical thoroughness in research and his talents as an analytical detective.

It was in 1940, shortly after I had completed the voluminous Competition among Grains, that a division chief in the U.S. Department of Agriculture invited me to work on the history of wheat—all the history of it, from the beginning of its cultivation until our days. I refused on the spot. Except for some familiarity with the history of cultivated plants (in the part pertaining to cereals or grains) in the more distant past and a somewhat greater familiarity with the developments in the relatively recent past, the topic, especially the work done by historians and linguists, was unfamiliar to me. But I thought: "Grain, including wheat, is the basis of economic life, the more so the further back one goes. History has been taught in every school of the world for hundreds of years. Hence everything must be known. If I undertake the job, it will be one, not of original research, but of compilation." The division chief had probably taken this for granted, but I was a little more ambitious.

Actually I was not in a position, financially, to be particularly selective. Some time later the financial pressure became so strong that I went to the man and told him: "O.K. If the job is still available, I shall do it." And he gave me an appointment for six months at a very low salary. (I am reluctant to ask what a job will pay, and in this case found it out only when it was financially impossible not to start working.)

Within a few days I was working enthusiastically. My assumption that everything was known turned out to be the error of the century. History, of course, existed all right. But my assumption turned out incorrect even with reference to such subjects as organization of the State and political developments—especially wars. The treatment of the problems I was interested in, namely grains, flours, breads in all aspects (production, processing, consumption, prices), left even much more to be desired. The exceptions were few and far between. An exception was first of all flour milling, specifically the grinding machines. R. Bennett and J. Elton (*History of Corn Milling*, Liverpool and London, 1898, four volumes) had published a very valuable investigation almost half a century before, and there was other valuable material on flour milling scattered over journals and books, as well as works on mills as such. Otherwise the principal exception, probably, was an English translation of Theophrastus by Sir Arthur Hort of Cambridge, published in two volumes in 1916. The list of plants compiled by Hort contained not less than fifty-six pages! It was a great pleasure to use his work. But while Hort's work was published by the Loeb Classical Library, the world center of classical literature, it does not seem to have been adequately used; one could say that it was frequently neglected in the subsequent publications of historians and classicists. Even less does this expertly written book seem to have spread the idea among wide circles of scholars, and especially publishers, that this is the only way of handling material requiring knowledge in special fields.

In general a lot of confusion was encountered. Not only different types of the same grain, but even individual grains as a whole, were not correctly distinguished. Emmer (the *zeia* and *olyra* of the Greeks; the *far* of the Romans) was a very important crop in classical antiquity—notably in the early period and even more in preclassical times. During some rather long periods, emmer probably dominated the grain production of Babylonia, Egypt, Rome, and possibly some other countries. The Greek names for this grain, given above, were correctly interpreted by Hort as emmer.* In spite of this, for years after his work was published, the practice continued of referring to this grain as spelt.† The enthusiastic description of the "famous" *alica* by Pliny has been reproduced time and again. Yet in Pliny's statement that *alica* was made from *far*, *alica* was translated as "spelt" as late as 1940.‡ The fact is, however, that *alica*, a very crude farina or semolina, could not have been made from spelt, a relatively mealy wheat. As far as hulled wheats are concerned, emmer, which is normally glassy, seems to have been the only suitable material for it.

Even more harmful for the analysis than the confusion about the name, was the fact that distinguished scholars either missed emmer completely or did not know what the grain was that they were talking about. Many, maybe all, did not realize that emmer is wheat, the same grain as that from which their everyday bread is made. Its only difference from the wheat they know is that in threshing, the kernels remain in the hulls.

Emmer (even under the name "spelt") does not occur at all in the big volume (732 pages) devoted by Professor A. C. Johnson to *Roman Egypt* (vol. 2 of *An Economic Survey of Ancient Rome*,

---

* I happened to know this from the history of cultivated plants before I ever heard of Hort.

† The translation of Pliny in the Loeb Classical Library, which was published in 1950, has emmer rather than spelt [*Natural History*, book 18]. I cherish the thought that this is one of the results of my efforts in *The Wheats of Classical Antiquity* (Baltimore, Md.: Johns Hopkins University Press, 1944). [Jasny is cited as the source for an explanation of *far* in *Der Kleine Pauly: Lexicon der Antike* (Stuttgart: Alfred Druckenmüller, 1967), 2:514.]

‡ See, for example, *An Economic History of Ancient Rome* (Baltimore, Md.: Johns Hopkins University Press, 1940), 5:135.

Baltimore, 1936). There were still sufficient amounts of emmer grown in Egypt in Pliny's time for him to know that "it threshed readily and produced a good yield" (Pliny *Natural History* 18. 93). Johnson probably missed this grain completely because he did not realize that behind some name unfamiliar to him was concealed the greatly preferred wheat, only in hulls.

Professor F. M. Heichelheim repeatedly referred to emmer as an inferior grain, while including barley among superior grains (see, for example, the section devoted to Syria in *An Economic Survey of Ancient Rome*, Tenney Frank, ed. [Baltimore, 1938], 4:129). He would not have done this had he realized that emmer is wheat.

The following phenomenon is of interest in this connection. In a long section devoted to naked wheat by Pliny (*Natural History* 18. 63–70), a statement is included that certain emmers weighed twenty-five or twenty-six pounds to the modius. The weights were obviously those of emmer with the hulls removed. The fact that Pliny did not consider it necessary to mention this fact indicates that a lot of emmer circulated in this form. The most important conclusion from what Pliny says of emmer in the place cited seems to be that hull-less emmer was treated as naked wheat. This statement by Pliny appears to be generally disregarded in historical literature, probably because the scholars do not know what to do with it. To clarify the situation fully, let it be added that emmer is the hulled wheat of the durum group (subspecies),* grown already in early antiquity. The first cultivated grain was probably barley, but emmer must have come close behind. The naked wheats of the durum group probably developed from emmer and not vice versa. Emmer came to Rome from the south or east. Spelt, on the other hand, is the hulled wheat of the common-wheat group, the most important of which is common wheat (*triticum vulgare*).† Spelt may be only a very few thousand years old, having been developed, possibly even in Europe, from the naked wheat when this—penetrating north and northwestward from Asia—met with adverse growing conditions. It came to Italy from the north, and in antiquity hardly penetrated as far south as the city of Rome.

---

* The naked wheats of the durum subspecies include, apart from durum proper (*triticum durum*), poulard wheat (*triticum turgidum*) and the very rare Polish wheat (*triticum polonicum*). Polish is a misnomer.

† The other naked wheats of this subspecies are club wheat (*triticum compactum*) and a rare wheat *triticum sphaerococcum*.

In the part of volume 4, p. 606, of *An Economic Survey of Rome*, devoted to Roman Asia Minor, *tiphe* (*titricum monococcum*, one-seeded **wheat**) is translated *secale*, which was rye. The author translated *kegkhros* as "sorghum" (it was millet), and the result was that sorghum turned up as the grain which dominated the plains of Pontus (the present South Russia), although sorghum is a crop of warmer climate and, in spite of having been mentioned by Pliny, was hardly ever grown in Europe.

Thus, barley may be the only grain which has not been confused with another grain by some author or translator.

While grains were not always identified properly, the situation was inevitably bad also with reference to more specialized items, such as different types of the same grain, or different products made from them.

There was, thus, plenty to do. The half-year appointment was prolonged for another half year. After that it was established that instead of perhaps ten thousand years, I had covered only about a thousand. So I was rated zero for "inability to accomplish an assignment," and dropped. To support my family I had to start at once on something entirely different (spreads between prices of grain and bread in the world at the present time). But I continued to work on antiquity during weekends and in the evenings. Then I had a spell of unemployment, devoting it entirely to antiquity. After this, again came weekend and evening work, until the exhaustion of accumulated material forced a definite discontinuation. This was the way in which there came into being the book *The Wheats of Classical Antiquity* (The Johns Hopkins University Studies in Historical and Political Science, Baltimore, 1944), the monograph "Wheat Prices and Milling Costs in Classical Rome" (in *Wheat Studies* of the Food Research Institute, Stanford, March, 1944), and the three other publications of mine on the subject.* The editor of *Isis* was not far off the mark when in a letter to me he called the subject my first love. It was not the first love, but it was a great love.

The total time I spent on my work on classical antiquity may seem immensely small, almost miraculously so. But miracles do not occur. Firstly, the work done is obviously incomplete to a very great

---

* "Competition among Grains in Classical Antiquity," *American Historical Review*, July, 1942; "The Breads of Ephesus and Their Prices," *Agricultural History*, July, 1947; and "The Daily Bread of the Ancient Greeks and Romans," *Osiris*, 1950.

extent and has unmistakable signs of haste, and secondly, my preceding work largely prepared me for the job. The five years I spent as a manager of a flour mill in 1909–1915 familiarized me with the grains (wheat, rye, and barley) and the milling techniques, and laid the foundation for my subsequent work on the world grain markets. Although not without interruptions, I had spent more than twenty years (not counting my sojourn at the flour mill) working on these markets before I turned my full attention to antiquity. Moreover, I was covering only the grains of the Occidental world—in substance the five grains: wheat, rye, barley, oats, and corn (maize).

The Pre- and Post-Classical Periods

While I had a rather extensive, and in some respects detailed, equipment for the work on the history of grain,* a considerable amount of additional knowledge had to be acquired. But first let me discuss the period covered. The assignment was to cover the history of wheat from the beginning of cultivation to our days. There were no insurmountable difficulties in covering the postclassical time, although the world is large, the period long (almost 1,500 years), and the material immense but by no means conclusive. A thorough coverage would require a lot of time. Still, given the time needed, I would have completed it. But this was unthinkable in the time available. So, after only a little work on the postclassical period, its continuation was postponed, as it turned out, forever.

It was quite different with reference to the period preceding classical antiquity, i.e., prior to about 500 B.C. (the classical period may be assumed to have lasted from about 500 B.C. to about A.D. 500). I devoted more time to the preclassical than to the postclassical period. I even spent a week in a famous Oriental institute, where I had discussions with the staff researchers and worked in the library. For some reason, possibly because grain growing is supposed to have started in Assyro-Babylonia, or its vicinity, I turned my attention first to this. There is a book by [Bedrich] Hrozny, *Das Getreide im alten Babylonien* [Grain in old Babylonia], Vienna, 1914. I read the book and was enchanted at what refined flours, malts, and beers men were able to prepare as far back as several thousands of years ago and at how much Hrozny knew from the inscriptions, which were inacces-

---

* The history of wheat can be worked successfully only in the frame of several other grains.

sible to me, about all those things. I read the book again and again, and the more I read, the more serious became my doubts. So I wrote to the above-mentioned institute and asked them what they could tell me about Hrozny's book. The answer was: Hrozny is a great expert in Assyro-Babylonian inscriptions, but you are the grain expert.

I was, and still am, very interested in the problem: how old is fermented bread? At least some experts in preclassical history seem to believe that fermented bread, as well as fermented beer, has existed for some five thousand years or more. I never found time to go into the problem of the age of beer, although the connection with fermented bread makes it essential. Still, in a preliminary way, I wanted, and still want, to place the development of fermented bread in the last millenium before Christ.* A passage in the translation of the Gilgamesh poem, Cambridge edition, seemed to refute my opinion fully. So a letter again went to the above-mentioned institute. The answer was at least as disheartening as the first: "The fact that something is in a translation of Gilgamesh does not necessarily mean that anything of that kind is in the original."

So, obviously, it was impossible to go on in this area with the expectation of getting results in a hurry. The director of the institute happened to be in Washington. I looked him up and tried to convey to him the impasse—his institute being able to read the sources but unable to interpret them because of lack of familiarity with the subjects themselves, and myself in the reverse position—and that for

---

* The description of preparation of "kneaded bread," obviously unleavened, in Cato (74) and his failure even to hint that any other than this "kneaded" bread existed, seems not to leave any doubt that this Roman senator, who lived in the second century B.C., did not know anything of leavened bread. Given the nature of his treatise, Cato would have said something if he had known. With the communications rather lively in the Mediterranean area, it seems improbable that a certain very important technique, known in Babylonia 3,000 years before Christ, did not reach Rome for some 2,800 years. In describing the preparation and use of leaven, Pliny (18. 105) reported that "people who live on fermented bread have weaker bodies, inasmuch as in the old days outstanding wholesomeness was ascribed to wheat the heavier it was." The idea is certainly not a testimony that good leavened bread had existed for a long time in the first century A.D., when Pliny lived. Pliny's information that the bread made in Gaul and Spain was lighter than the others (18. 68) because they used the "foam" obtained in beer preparation as a leaven, also does not testify to a well-developed and long-established technique of making leavened bread. Good leavened bread was prepared later without the use of the "foam."

fruitful work it was desirable at some future time (the conversation took place during World War II) to bring both fields of knowledge together. But the director was not interested.

So the topic to be worked on was cut from both ends and limited to a matter of "only" about 1,000 years, the classical era. To limit in this way the study for the time being seemed advisable also because by that time I had familiarized myself a little with the handling of the subject in the publications written by general historians and experts in classical languages, and believed myself to be able to suggest significant improvements. My original idea that everything was known was of course absurd. The degree of perfection visualized by me may, indeed, never be attained. But the treatment of the topic needs also not to be as dilettante as it turned out to be, especially with reference to such indispensable items as bread and the grain and the flour from which it is made.

The territory covered was stripped of its outskirts. My work was practically confined to the Mediterranean region, which was the center of the world in those days. This simplified the task also in that only wheat and barley, the two grains which played a great role in the Mediterranean region, needed to be given major consideration.

I, of course, proceeded on the assumption that in real research (there is a lot of quasi-research, especially in government offices) nothing should be taken over uncritically. I was therefore desperate to restrict the subject to a scope possible to handle critically within the limited time available.

The Special Job

As shown, I had some preparation for the job. It is, for example, impossible to exaggerate the importance of the little botany I knew (it would be more exact to speak of a more or less thorough familiarity with the grains grown now, which included a little knowledge of botany). When I read in Columella (2. 16), "There is a second variety of barley which some call *distichum*," well, I know what *distichum* barley is.

The finding that Pliny's *triticum* and Columella's *robus* were naked wheats of the durum group also simplified analysis greatly. At least one knew that it was not *triticum vulgare*. A considerable uncertainty remained, it is true, due to the inability to decide definitely— on the basis of the descriptions by Pliny, Columella, and other ancient authors—which sorts in the group were durum wheat proper and which were poulards.*

Still, further fields of knowledge, or deepenings of knowledge, were indispensable for the special job in hand. There is always some minimum ground which needs to be covered to accomplish a research job successfully. I knew, for example, that the Mediterranean area, including Asia Minor and Syria, had the Mediterranean climate and that Mediterranean climate means winter rain and summer drought, but this was about all I knew—working in the wide frame of the whole Occidental world. Much more detailed knowledge of the climate was required. The situation was similar with reference to soils.†

A thorough study of the climate and soil of the countries and portions of the countries comprising the classical world seemed especially necessary as a guide, since the other sources were by no means conclusive; indeed, they were often misleading. In this connection I recall a visit to one of the most prominent classicists in the U.S.A. He found insufficient knowledge of classical sources on my part and dismissed me on this account. My attempt to explain that the classical sources were to me not *the* sources but only *among* the sources and that it seemed to me more advantageous first to get a picture of the climate and soil of the areas involved was not crowned

---

* It is worth mentioning that several years before the publication of Pliny's Book 18, by the Loeb Classical Library, I offered to the American publishers of the library my assistance in the translating of a few paragraphs from this book (for a thank you, of course), but was refused. On second thoughts, it was for the best. I am still struggling with those few paragraphs of Pliny which deal with grain and flour. There is a great deal in them that I do not understand. Not only do I by-pass statements which I am unable to interpret, but on occasions I act contrary to Pliny's expressly made statement. In 18. 62, Pliny said that barley was lighter than emmer. On the basis of what is known of these grains, supported by ample Egyptian evidence, I assume that, as harvested, barley was perhaps 50% heavier than emmer. Like his modern translator, Pliny was by no means an expert on all the various items he dealt with. He might well have mixed up the evidence pertaining to emmer without hulls with that for emmer in hulls. Such statements as *"tritico nihil est fertilius"* ("Nothing exceeds wheat in prolificness"—Pliny 18. 94) contradicts all that we know about yields of the different kinds of grain in all the world. I believe it possible that Italian wheat was superior to foreign wheats in whiteness (Pliny 18. 63), but he also claimed that it excelled in weight, which is difficult to visualize. This writer does not believe himself able always to distinguish the correct from the incorrect in Pliny and some other classical authors.

† In works by historians and, especially, by classicists, the word "climate," or anything else connected with it, is rarely found in the indexes.

with much success. Later on, having seen my published work, the professor found merit in it, however.

The study of the climate of the area involved did not present any difficulties whatever. It was only necessary to ascertain that—say around Christ's time—the climate of the area involved was not significantly different from the present one, and reference books provided all the evidence necessary. Yet this easily acquired evidence proved invaluable. It is, for example, very important for the competition of barley with wheat (to some extent also of naked wheat with emmer, the hulled wheat) that the average annual precipitation is high (slightly over 800 millimetres) in Rome, but low (slightly less than 400 millimetres) in Athens, and that the rainy season is much shorter in the latter. These differences alone may suffice to explain (and if they cannot explain fully, they were certainly very important factors) the fact that at the time of Demosthenes and Plato, Athens grew barley almost exclusively, with naked wheat a very distant second. The area around Rome, however, at the same time probably grew naked and hulled wheat, or hulled and naked wheat, with a certain amount of barley grown mainly on lighter soils. It is simply impossible to draw a map of the distribution of the various grains in the Mediterranean region, if the map is not overlaid (at least in imagination) with maps showing precipitation and soil.

The only book on Mediterranean soils that was located was in Spanish. Moreover, the title "Mediterranean Soils" had the addition "as illustrated by Spanish Soils." Without familiarity with the language, it was of course quite a task to extract some knowledge from the book (it helped, though, that the names of soils are largely international, and there was a lady available who translated to me passages which I could not handle myself with a dictionary). A very good investigation of Tunisian soils could have been studied. A study of the soils of Asia Minor was also found.

Soils are largely the product of the climate. So, familiarity with the climate helped me to understand the soils.

For familiarity with the grains, flours, and breads, the technical practices employed in the preparation and their uses, etc., in classical times, one had to turn to classical sources.

I had eight years of Latin and six years of Greek in school, but I did not acquire much knowledge even then, and in the ensuing forty years or so—until the time I could have used some of it—almost all of what I did acquire, especially the Greek, had disappeared. It was absolutely impossible to get a reading knowledge of the two languages (I did not succeed in this even at school) in the time at my disposal for the new project. So, I had to resort to translations (fortunately, almost everything important had been translated). But, with rare exceptions—perhaps only that of Sir Arthur Hort, the translator of Theophrastus—the rendering of special terms in translations of classical authors in this field can not be made the basis of an analysis; they can only mislead. Examples of mistreatment of grains have been given above.*

The seemingly great difficulty with the translations was overcome by a preliminary study of the special terms (Greek and Latin) important for my analysis (names of grains, flours, etc.) and by using thereafter translations with the original text on the facing pages and looking up the original text, whenever one of the special terms came along. The method worked fine. There was only one case when I was about to be sunk due to unfamiliarity with the language. In the translation of Pliny which preceded the one in the Loeb Classical Library, the phrase "white wheat" occurred; it fitted badly in my ideas on the wheat in question, but "white" is "white," and nothing could be done about this, it seemed. Miss Elsa Rose Graser, then connected with the Johns Hopkins University (she translated the Edict of Diocletian for volume 5 of *An Economic Survey of Ancient Rome*, ed. by T. Frank), saved me. I am happy to use this opportunity to make this specific acknowledgment (general credit to her was given in my book). In reading one of my earliest drafts, she said to me: "You know, the word which in the volume is translated "white" may also mean "shining." Well, this is a world of difference. White (wheat) most probably means the subspecies *triticum vulgare* (indeed, probably *triticum vulgare* proper) but "shining"!—this is the durum group, probably *triticum durum* proper (the best durum wheat is now customarily sold as "amber durum"). When next I met "white wheat" in a famous translation of the Mishnah, I just ran to the Semetic division of the Library of Congress, asked the man in charge to find the word translated as "white" in the original and tell me whether the word can also be translated "shining," or something similar—i.e., opposite to "dull." The suspicion turned out to

---

* It is worth mentioning that the expert Hort left more words untranslated than the nonexperts who have translated Pliny. Leaving words untranslated impairs readability, but it greatly increases the usefulness of the translations for research.

be correct. The area with which the Mishnah dealt was unlikely to have grown any naked wheat but durum.

The situation described here is not exceptional but rather general. Most of my life has been spent in agricultural economics. It is difficult to find an agricultural economist who realizes that for dealing with many problems in his field, familiarity with the technical background (soil, climate, machinery, agronomy) is indispensable. I recollect an agricultural economist, and a very good one, who for perhaps twenty years worked on cotton, but was frank enough to state that he did not know anything on the warmth requirements of the plant.

The Findings

It is not the intention of the present writer to review in any detail even his major findings on grain, flour, bread, and some related factors (especially the prices of grain) in classical antiquity. Only a few points will be discussed briefly.

From the technical side, the work done is possibly best described as a synthesis—a synthesis of the findings on the history of cultivated plants, made mostly by botanists on the basis of such material as excavations, without full, or even any, consideration of the literary sources. These findings were combined with what I myself—fortified by familiarity with climate and soil of the areas involved and with milling techniques and other processing of grain and with the uses made of them—could extract from the classical sources, utilizing of course the interpretations made before me.

Living standards. A reviewer of my *The Wheats of Classical Antiquity* emphasized the most general point which can be made on the basis of my work.* He said that the book was a step forward in bringing realism into history. If my memory does not fail me, he spoke of elimination of romanticism from history.

The exaltation of antiquity, the ascription to antiquity of attainments made hundreds and thousands of years later, is apparent in much of the ground I covered. Professor Humfrey Michell, for example, in his book *The Economics of Ancient Greece*, Cambridge, England, 1940 (of which he said in the preface that he endeavored

---

* What a pity to have misplaced the most favorable review of any of my books, I do not even remember the name of the reviewer or the journal in which the review was published.

to give, in short compass, the results of modern research)—in describing the preparation of bread, which included the process of grinding—said: "to separate the flour from the bran the meal was sieved or 'bolted'" (p. 194), although maza, the standard grain food of the Greeks, was made from unsifted barley meal. Michell informed his readers that "all kinds of confectionery, fancy cakes, and pastry were made; we even know the name of one famous confectioner," he said, yet he neglected to mention the maza. What little bread was made by the Greeks in the time of their glory was referred to by Michell as loaves, although it was probably unleavened cakes. All in all, it is difficult to distinguish between the description of bread given by Michell for ancient Greece and one for the time when he was writing his book.

The same Michell wrote (p. 195): "Any idea that the high thinking of the Greeks was accompanied by plain living, at least among the better-to-do, may be dismissed at once." The important thing is, however, that the level for the better-to-do was quite different in classical Greece from what it is now. The same Athenaeus whom Michell quotes as evidence wrote (Deipnosophistae 4. 141) about the occasional voluntary contributions to the Spartan mess of epaikla, consumed as a delicacy after the dinner: "Sometimes the common people bring whatever is caught in the chase; but the rich contribute wheat bread"—wheat bread as dessert, as a delicacy. One had to be rich to contribute it occasionally to the mess. Socrates, a stonecutter, always went barefoot (Plato Phaedrus 220a); he put sandals on only once, on a very special occasion (Plato Symposium 174a).*

When a change in history is recognized by modern scholars, the duration of the transitional period is frequently visualized in time horizons normal for our days, but much too short for antiquity. Changes which occurred in one city (Athens, Rome), and may have nevertheless required decades, are ascribed to whole countries (Greece, Italy), where in the past they mostly took centuries and even millennia.

Neither a Greek nor a Roman source seems to have stressed or even mentioned the need for a thorough cleaning of the grain before the grinding to flour—an operation which is an essential part of modern flour production. The Egyptian mummies show teeth rubbed down by the sand in the bread they ate. The mummies may date

---

* Citations from Plato are from Bollingen series, vol. 71, 1961.

from preclassical times, but great improvements in this matter from preclassical to classical times are not indicated.

The "sand-clock" Roman mill turned by two men or a blind-folded donkey was an extremely imperfect implement. The flour obtained by it must have been of very poor quality, and the cost of grinding relatively high (for the type of flour produced). The great deficiency of the rotating stone mill explains why the hand-operated mortar was still extensively used in Pliny's time. The maza, of which the sources seem not to leave any doubt that it was the standard food from grain in Athens in the time of its glory and that it was made from *unsifted* barley meal, must have been a very poor foodstuff. According to a Greek source, maza was even not baked, but "dried on the fire" (apparently for only a few minutes). A noted dietician on the faculty of a great American university in a conversation with me flatly refused to believe that consumption by humans of a product from unsifted barley meal was possible.

The food made from grain was considerably better in Rome than in Greece. A large part of it was made from wheat.* Shortly before the time of Pliny a shift had been made to leavened bread. But white bread was a rarity even then. A plebeian did not get a slice of it even when, perhaps once in a lifetime, he was invited to dinner by his patron (Juvenal *Satires* 5. 70). Bread was made in Rome also from bran (*Panis furfureus*) and by no means for dietetic reasons. In the household of Cato the Elder, bread was baked, instead of in an oven, under a pot, with charcoal heaped over it. A world of change has occurred since that time in almost everything.

My conclusions as to the poorness of life in classical antiquity were based almost exclusively on analysis of the grain and grain products and of the literature primarily concerned with them (Hesiod, Theophrastus, Aristotle, Cato, Varro, Columella, Pliny, and some others). Lack of time made it impossible to study classical sources of a more general character. In a similar manner, publications dealing with classical antiquity in a much wider scope than mine were consulted only to a very inadequate extent. So I overlooked Plato, who, as it turns out, was a decisive source with reference to Greek life at the time when the high point of its culture was reached. I also overlooked a very valuable book which used the evidence of Plato among others, and which would have been of great help. It was already in

---

* There is of course also a time lag of a few hundred years.

its fifth edition at the time I was engaged in the work. I got hold of the volume only in 1962, when preparing this story. The book is Alfred Zimmern, *The Greek Commonwealth*. Citations here are, with one exception, from the first paperback edition, Oxford University Press, 1961 (how encouraging it is to see such a wide circulation!). My statements above on Socrates walking barefoot could be made only after my attention to Plato had been drawn by Zimmern. I am happy to say that the neglect of Zimmern and Plato did not cause any error on my part. Still I would have liked to have had the evidence in due time.

Zimmern speaks of "the incredible poverty" of Periclean Greece of the fifth century B.C. (p. 214). He elaborates as follows (p. 215): "It is easy to think away railways and telegraphs and gasworks and tea and advertisements and bananas. But we must peel off far more than this. We must imagine houses without drains, beds without sheets or springs, rooms as cold, or as hot, as the open air, only draughtier, meals that began and ended with pudding. . . ."

What Zimmern calls "pudding" was maza, of which we know well what poor stuff it was. Zimmern (p. 50) said of it: "The barley [obviously after coarse grinding or stamping in the mortar] was kneaded but not baked, and eaten as a sort of porridge with water."

Most illuminating is Plato's description of life in the ideal city in his *Republic* 372b and 372c. He wrote there (this is not Zimmern's translation):

> They will sustain themselves, preparing meal [alphita, whole barley meal] from barley grains, and flour [aleura, whole wheat meal] from wheat grains, and when they have baked the one and kneaded the other, they will serve noble cakes [maza in the original], and loaves, on a reed mat or clean leaves [in the text "noble" pertains only to the maza, but some scholars think the text corrupt and "noble" originally pertained to the loaves also].

Poorly prepared whole barley meal a noble food!

Everything eaten in the ideal city besides maza and wheat bread was either relish or dessert. Relish included, in addition to salt, onions, olives, greens, and—the only animal product served even during a feast—cheese. About dessert Plato said: "And for dessert we will serve them figs and chickpeas,* beans and they will toast myrtle ber-

---

* Chickpeas, if the word was correctly translated, is not believed to be usable as food in most of the world now.

ries and acorns before the fire, washing them down with moderate potations."* Chickpeas and beans as dessert!

On clothes, Plato said (*Republic* 372a): "In the ideal city people will be for the most part barefoot and naked in the summer, sufficiently shod and dressed in the winter."

Barley or wheat. Of specified problems of the type described, the competition between wheat and barley was given considerable attention in my work. Barley may be preferred to wheat as feed for animals in spite of the higher nutritive value of the latter. As food for humans, barley is definitely inferior to wheat, especially in competition with fermented wheat bread. If barley is grown for food *in quantity*, it is because the people *cannot afford* the burden of the inferiority of wheat as a farm crop as compared with barley. Barley has a shorter growing period than wheat, and moreover, it makes a much faster start immediately after seeding, when moisture is normally more plentiful. This is the reason why barley may completely escape the effect of a midsummer drought which would ruin a wheat crop. Even in terms of weight the yield of barley per acre is therefore normally larger or much larger than that of wheat. The competition of barley with wheat is particularly strong in areas of Mediterranean climate, due largely to the seasonal distribution of precipitation but also because barley thrives more than wheat in alkaline, neutral, or only slightly acid soils, the typical soils of the areas of Mediterranean climate. Lighter soils, widespread in the Mediterranean region, also are better adapted to barley than wheat.

One familiar with the growing conditions required by barley and with the distribution of barley-growing now and in the near past, for which reliable evidence is available, expects off-hand that in the classical world—largely confined to areas of Mediterranean climate— barley, say two thousand years ago, was much more important than it is now (or than it has been in the recent past); that in several countries with Mediterranean climate it is likely to have been the dominant grain crop, and where it was not dominant, it was a close second crop to wheat. Such an analyst is not the least surprised to find that in the historical literature the classical world is described as the world of wheat, with barley only a distant second. In a 106-page study devoted to the economy of Roman Spain in *An Economic Survey of Ancient Rome* (Tenney Frank, ed.), exactly four indifferent lines are devoted to barley (3:176).

---

* It was customary in Greece to drink wine diluted.

With the growing conditions (climate, soil) quite disregarded, the analysis in the historical literature is naturally based on classical sources, and this means largely Roman sources. But the Romans were the conquerors of the world and could more easily than anybody else afford to eat the more expensive wheat. They grew relatively more of it than they otherwise would have done and also naturally tried to squeeze from the dependent areas wheat rather than barley, even when little was produced of the former, even where the wheat may have had to be produced instead of barley for the specific purpose of delivering it to Rome. So it came about that in trade and tribute the role of wheat was several times greater than its role in total production. Since trade and tribute play a considerable part in what was written about, classical sources tended to present an incorrect picture on this ground too.

Even such a fact that naked wheat was usually mentioned ahead of barley in the sources has frequently affected present-day analysis, although this practice obviously was not due necessarily to the extent of growing, but was brought about by the high esteem for naked wheat, for its greater role in trade and tribute, etc. In any novel, Sunday is likely to be mentioned more frequently than each individual weekday.

The olive tree is a specialty of the Mediterranean climate, and so is, to a large extent, wine. The idea that wheat was the dominant grain in the Mediterranean region in antiquity led to the creation of the attractive formula that the triad—wheat, wine, and olives—was the mainstay of classical antiquity.

I was not a little surprised to find the statement repeated as late as 1962, in a book devoted to, of all places, Mycenae (The Mycenaeans lived on the Greek mainland in the second millenium B.C.) and the Minoans (who lived on the island of Crete at about the same time).*

In addition to the statement "the chief staple agricultural products of the Mediterranean world, wheat, olive oil and wine naturally figure prominently in our texts" (it is on p. 102 of Palmer's book), we find on p. 17 the statement "we need nothing to convince us of the importance of wheat, wine, oil and cattle in Mycenaean

* Leonard R. Palmer, *Mycenaeans and Minoans: Aegean Prehistory in the Light of the Linear B Tablets* (New York: Knopf, 1963), p. 102. The Linear B tablets were discovered only very recently. An immense, indeed revolutionary, importance is assigned to them for this history of preclassical Greece.

Greece." Yet the tablet in Figure 19, p. 116, as interpreted by Palmer, shows that the grain rations were issued in barley to slaves, handicraft workers, cult personnel, and even "an exalted social class." It is impossible for me to study all the materials pertaining to the Linear B tablets, and I am certainly not an expert in interpreting inscriptions like those involved here; but it seems that the following remarks have sufficient justification.

It is open to question whether one should approach the situation on the Greek mainland and Crete in the second millenium B.C. with a formula covering all Mediterranean countries in a later period, and to ignore the fact that in any case in the territory with which Palmer is concerned, the situation in this later time was quite different. It would seem that if Palmer had not approached his material with the idea that wheat was the staple grain crop of the Mediterranean world, ignoring altogether the proved fact that several centuries later barley, and not wheat, was the staple grain crop in the very territory he dealt with, his tablets may well have led to quite different conclusions. That Palmer expected to find wheat rather than barley in his tablets is obivous from the adjective "naturally" in the statement on p. 102, and from the form of the statement on p. 17.*

While wheat dominated the classical world according to the historical literature, one may be certain of this only with reference to the vicinity of Rome (by no means the whole of Italy; and even in the area of Rome, not in the early part of the classical period) as well as in Egypt—in the latter case due to the greater gain of wheat from artificial irrigation, which is another factor needing attention when considering the competition among various grains grown in antiquity or any other time.†

---

* Palmer's book, pp. 58–60, contains a long glossary of signs, deciphered in the tablets he dealt with. The glossary contains an interpretation of signs for almost twenty crops, including such rare ones as coriander. Yet no sign was discovered for emmer. Pylos, the capital of the Mycenaeans, the place where the tablets were found, was located on the western side of the Peloponnesus. The abundance of precipitation there makes it very probable that if wheat was grown by the Myceanaeans at all, it was exclusively or mainly emmer. It seems that those working on the tablets did not look for a sign for emmer. The case of emmer is another indication that work on the tablets was done without sufficient familiarity with the grains grown in antiquity.

† If it is true that "the normal crop was common wheat" in Roman Britain (R. G. Collingwood, "Roman Britain," in An Economic Survey of Ancient Rome, vol. 3 [Baltimore, Md.: Johns Hopkins University Press, 1937],

The specific growing conditions favoring rye are not encountered in the Mediterranean area. It was probably grown in any quantity in antiquity only in a part of Asia Minor and in such outside parts of the Mediterranean area as the northern Balkans or the southern Alps. Millet, unadapted to the Mediterranean climate and particularly adapted to conditions of a nomadic population of warm areas with summer precipitation, dominated the present South Russia. In the Mediterranean region proper, apart from wheat there was only barley as a candidate for a major role in grain growing, and it is my opinion that, next to Greece, for which classical sources make it certain, barley dominated grain production in Africa (Tunisia, Algeria, Morocco), Syria and Palestine, Spain, and probably Babylonia, and was also very important in Sicily, Apulia, and Calabria.

In general, I devoted considerable space to arguing that people grew and necessarily ate, not what they liked, but largely what they could more easily produce. This observation is still valid now. The fact is particularly pronounced in such underdeveloped countries as India. The consumers as distinct from the producers play much too great a role in historical literature for the analysts to reach reliable conclusions.

Flour extraction rates. Professor L. A. Moritz* gave me a lot of credit for my analysis of Pliny's data on flour extractions. Here the same problem is involved as that which appeared in dealing with the prices of emmer (and spelt), namely, the difficulty arising even for great historians from their inability to handle such a pedestrian thing as the measuring of produce in terms of volume. Because of the presence of a great deal of hull in the grain as harvested, emmer,

---

p. 78), there must have been a substantial reversal in later times, when Britain grew also barley, oats, rye, even possibly spelt and/or emmer. Also, in later times for which records are available, Britain produced a good deal of poulard wheat (which as material for bread is inferior to common wheat). It is implied in the statements of Collingwood that this, too, must have been introduced after the time on which Collingwood reported. For Collingwood's assertions proofs would be desirable. Like Professor Palmer and others, he may have been too much influenced by the wrong idea that wheat dominated the Mediterranean world in classical time. On the other hand, the word "common" in Collingwood's statement may not have been meant in the botanical sense. He may have meant poulard wheat, using the term "common wheat" in a historical sense.

* *Grain-Mills and Flour in Classical Antiquity* (Oxford: Oxford University Press, 1958).

although intrinsically more valuable than barley, was cheaper than the latter when sold, as was customary, by volume, and it has therefore erroneously been classed as inferior to barley.

Connected with the extraction rates of the various flours is the simple fact, likewise not realized by historians, that wheat, after having been ground to whole-wheat meal, occupies more space than the wheat from which it is made. This addition was estimated by me at about 20–25%.*

Hardly any credit is due to me for the analysis of the extractions. All I did was to apply the knowledge possessed by everyone in a mill, or in a business dealing with grain or grain products, to the specific case of Pliny's data on flour extraction.

Future Work

A major reason for writing this account is to draw attention to the fact that general historians or linguists should not, so far as can be avoided, have to handle problems requiring special knowledge outside their own fields. Special problems must be placed in the hands of specialists.† In many cases this would suffice. Every intelligent man connected with grain grinding should be able to handle correctly problems arising from the fact that in antiquity, as also much later, grain and grain products were measured not by weight but by volume. (The present units for measuring grain—quarters, bushels, etc.—are a vivid reminder of that not distant time.)

But on frequent occasions the specialist must accommodate himself to the idea that he is dealing with the distant past, that while some items may have remained as they were (for example the grains grown have hardly changed), other things have mostly changed greatly, such as grain grinding, flours, breads. Time and again in-

---

* This statement is made on the basis of existing practices. The specific weights calculated in Table 2 in *Isis* indicate that in antiquity, or just in Rome at Pliny's time, the flour was packed less tightly than it is now. The absence of data on the tightness of packing the flour, on the water retention of the bread, and other such technicalities are just some of the uncertainties with which one has to deal.

† Conway Zirkle in a review of my *The Wheats of Classical Antiquity* (*Isis*, May, 1947, p. 96) is of the same opinion. He wrote: "Their [the classical authors'] records are of such a nature that they have to be studied by experts in several fields before they can be interpreted accurately." Some other reviewers expressed the same opinion.

ability to transfer oneself into the situation of two or three thousand years ago is observed, even in the works of great professional historians.

Professor Moritz has devoted much space in support of the probability that the Romans practiced repeated grinding (see pp. 158–59, 178), and in this he based his conclusions on the experiments made for him in a laboratory. Yet some classical writer, especially Pliny, would most probably have mentioned this very important detail in unmistakable terms (remember the detailed description of sieves, even with their names, in Pliny).*

It seems that Professor Moritz, and his advisers, are not clear on the very technical and easily overlooked problem of the fineness of the flour produced in antiquity. The primitiveness of the mills and especially the expensiveness of the power employed is likely to have precluded production of flours even approaching the present-day flour in fineness. Flour of a fineness approaching that of the present time probably began to be established only after a sufficient perfection of the water mill, which did not occur before the Middle Ages.

In addition to the discussion in my book on ancient wheat prices, I dealt a little with the primitive grinding of grain and specifically the coarseness of the flour produced in antiquity, prior to it, and also in our days, in "The Daily Bread of the Ancient Greeks and Romans," *Osiris* (Bruges, 1950).† I tried to show that the productivity especially of saddle-stone and rotating handmills was very small, in spite of the crudeness of the flour produced. At the moment I can only add a very rough calculation of the work of a Roman mill rotated by two men walking around it.‡ The two men together are unlikely to have developed more than one-sixth of one horsepower per hour, if that, and to have worked more than eight hours net. Hence, total power developed by them during the workday was equal to about 1.3 horsepower hours. One horsepower now grinds in an hour about thirty pounds of grain to flour of thinness normal for the present time. Hence if the two men rotating the Roman mill would have

---

* In 18. 115, Pliny states that a spurious *alica*, after having been pounded, is divided in four sizes by employment of three sieves (*farinarium, secundarium, angustissimum*). This is the process that may well have been involved also in Pliny's three-grade flour grindings.

† Unfortunately, Professor Moritz did not apparently see this article.

‡ The work of a blindfold donkey moving in a very small circle around the stone is unlikely to have been much cheaper. Otherwise, men would not have been used as extensively as was done to turn the mills.

been grinding as thinly as modern grinding, the output of the mill would have been not more than forty pounds per day. While I do not expect the Roman mill to have had a large output, forty pounds per day may still be much too low. It would mean that a town with 10,000 population would need more than 200 mills (of course the mills may have been operated in two or three shifts), and about every twelfth or fifteenth adult man would have pulled a mill every weekday. The "flour" of the Romans was probably a mixture of fine flour, intermediate products, and really large pieces, as it still is in one-passage grinding today.

Concluding Remarks

The encouragement for my work on classical antiquity in the U.S.A. was mixed. In the early stages of this work I visited, among others, Michael Rostovtzev, the famous investigator of the Hellenistic era, who, after having become an emigrant, found refuge in Yale University. After I had informed him of what I had found and what line I intended to pursue, he said about as follows: "For years I hoped that a man with your background would come and help us solve the problems we are unable to deal with ourselves," proving by this awareness of his own limitations what a great scholar he was.

I shall be permitted to indulge in the pleasure of quoting somewhat more from the reviews of my book on the wheats of classical antiquity. Conway Zirkle (*Isis*, May, 1947, p. 96) wrote as follows: "The author of this small book is obviously a linguist and a classicist and he is not unacquainted with agriculture and modern botany. He is thus excellently equipped for the task he has undertaken"; the author "is clearly competent in enough fields to make a contribution beyond the power of any narrow specialist. This he has done."

George F. Carter, in *Quarterly Review of Biology* (vol. 21, no. 3 [September, 1946], pp. 286–87), who considered me "a practical agronomist," wrote: "Jasny was able to make unusual use of such information [information contained in classical sources]. His insight into milling methods, the characteristics of flour from various wheats, the losses in milling, etc., as well as his close knowledge of the growth habits of the various varieties of wheat and the new divisions of wheat based on genetic knowledge, made it possible for him to squeeze a great deal of meaning out of what at first sight seems scanty and unsatisfactory material."

Jean Catrysse in *L'Antiquité Classique* (vol. 15 [1946], phase 2, pp. 352–53), apparently ascribed my handling of the topic, which the reviewer believed successful, to my being a "botanist."

Thus an economist was described as a "linguist," "classicist," "practical agronomist," and "botanist."* It shows that the neighboring sciences were not badly treated by the economist.†

The professional press was very kind to me. It amply rewarded me for my effort and amply compensated for the lack of understanding shown in some circles—specifically for the zero rating "for inability to accomplish an assignment" made by the U.S. Department of Agriculture.

---

* The unfamiliarity with my study of wheat prices in classical Rome, of course, contributed much to my displacement. But the very fact of displacement is pleasing.

† But I am reasonably certain I could have made more progress in interpreting some of the many varieties of the various grains, at least of their subspecies, mentioned by the classical authors, if I really were a botanist or had had advice from a competent botanist. I am by no means certain, for example, that the line between durums and poulards was drawn correctly. I have never been on a farm for more than a couple of hours, but probably knew enough of the agronomy of grain for my task. As concerns the "linguist and classicist," they were substituted by research experience. The fact that nobody recognized me for what I really was (a cereal economist with some familiarity in neighboring sciences) is still amusing, although it may have been caused by a somewhat one-sided selection of publications to which my book was sent for review by the publisher. Or did the publisher not expect understanding for this type of work on the part of economic journals? There would be something in this.

7—Free Lance and Bias

WORLD WAR II

Shortly after Naum Jasny commenced his research into the history of wheat, his father, Michael, succeeded finally in immigrating to the United States. Although he was eighty-two years old and virtually penniless (he was carrying his last possession of any value, a box of silverware), the senior Jasny was determined to initiate a new career by opening another automat in New York. Neither his age nor the lack of means with which to establish a business seemed to discourage the indomitable old gentleman. After staying briefly with Simon, Michael moved into Naum's small Washington apartment and continued making plans for his automat.

The following spring (1941), Tanya completed her M.A. in social work and married an economist, Milton Moss, who, after their marriage, found employment at the Federal Reserve Bank in Washington. Michael visited them when they were furnishing their first apartment and insisted on helping Tanya's husband construct a bookcase. However, woodworking was not Michael's forte, and in planing the shelves, he worked against the grain, leaving permanent furrows in the wood which are still pointed out affectionately by his granddaughter.

Unfortunately, Michael was never to realize his plan of opening an automat in New York, for in 1942, after eighty-four years of vigorous activity, his exhausted heart ceased, and the grand old man and his ambitions were laid to rest in the city which he had hoped would hold his future.

With the entry of the United States into World War II, one would have expected Naum Jasny's talents to be in considerable demand. Apparently, however, this was not the case.

During World War II, when Stalin was the ally of the U.S.A., the people in the U.S.A. interested in the Soviet economy who took a definite stand against all kinds of dictatorship, including of course Stalin's, could be counted on the fingers of one hand, and this caused for me a number of difficulties. I was actually unemployed for some time. There certainly was nobody as qualified for work on Soviet agriculture for the war effort as I was, yet I was refused a job by the Russian Division of the OSS (Office of Strategic Services)—the center for such work. I ultimately landed a job in the FEA (Foreign Economic Administration), but to cover West European agriculture and on a per diem basis.

To be technically correct, we should point out here that Jasny actually was employed—probably in the summer of 1942—by the Board of Economic Warfare (formerly the Economic Defense Board), which, along with several other offices, was consolidated the following year into the Foreign Economic Administration. According to Mrs. Luba Richter, Jasny remained with that organization until it was terminated at the end of September, 1945, and its functions were redistributed among the departments of State, Commerce, and Agriculture. At that time Jasny returned to the Agriculture Department.[1]

During the war years, Jasny produced three monographs for the Department of Agriculture and a number of articles on European agriculture for the Journal of Farm Economics and for the U.S.D.A. publication Foreign Agriculture. These included three on Soviet agriculture specifically. He also returned briefly to his great love, classical grains, for a two-page item in Agricultural History called "The Breads of Ephesus and Their Prices."

During World War II, with a miniature staff,* I was covering the agriculture of Europe including the U.S.S.R. for the FEA (Foreign Economic Administration). In reading some extracts from Soviet

---

* Foremost among those who were helping me in the FEA was Mrs. Luba Richter, who since then has made a great research career of her own in the U.S. State Department. Very useful also was the assistance of Mrs. Helen Bevans, whose work as an economic analyst started under me (this can probably be said also of Mrs. Richter) and who after a few years became an independent analyst.

newspapers, I came across the statement that in 1939, 13.9 percent of the kolkhoz grain harvest was used for feed. Interesting, but nothing much could be done with the information, because neither the amount produced nor that fed to animals was known. The situation would be quite different, I thought, if, instead of the amount fed, the evidence—although in percentage terms—involved an item which could be estimated at least roughly. Fortunately, the information contained a reference to an issue of *Izvestiya*. When we procured the issue, it contained the invaluable evidence of A. Arina on the distribution of the 1939–1940 kolkhoz grain crop by the various uses (obligatory deliveries, payments to the MTS [Machine Tractor Station], etc.) in percentage terms. Later his similar data for 1937–1938 and 1938–1939 were located. By substituting for the percentages the official data on the distribution of grain in payment for workdays to collective farmers, the estimated utilization for seed and for some other items, and by using semiofficial statements on the relation of the grain crops of 1935 and 1936 to that of 1937, reasonably exact estimates of the kolkhoz grain crops in 1935–1939 could be made for those years. The estimating of the small grain output of the sovkhozy did not present such difficulties. So I had fairly reliable estimates of the total grain crops in 1935–1939.*[2] I do not know whether I would have started the tedious work on the *Socialized Agriculture* book if not for the certainty that the reconstructed data of Arina would give me a firm hold on the situation in Soviet agriculture during the pre-World War II part of the industrialization drive.

Building on the agricultural data published by A. Arina, Jasny expanded his study to cover large-scale state and collectivized peasant farming, thus finding the focus for his next major undertaking.³

A NEW DIRECTION

In September, 1945, when the FEA was terminated, Jasny returned to the Department of Agriculture as a staff member of the Office of Foreign Agricultural Relations. By then he must have been deeply committed to his study of socialized agriculture and seeking outside financial help so that he could pursue it full time.

Early in 1946 the Food Research Institute at Stanford, under Dr.

* See *The Socialized Agriculture of the USSR*, table 60 on p. 738, and the accompanying text.

M. K. Bennett, acknowledged the value of Jasny's project and agreed to subsidize him to a limited extent.[4] In late 1947 Jasny retired from the U.S.D.A., signed a contract with the Food Research Institute to serve as its Washington representative, and launched into full-time work on what was to become his monumental study, The Socialized Agriculture of the USSR: Plans and Performance. Fortunately, the funds provided by the institute (underwritten to a significant degree by the Rockefeller Foundation),[5] plus his pension and Social Security payments, were enough to permit Jasny to continue his research on a free-lance basis.[6]

Independence allowed him to follow his own personal schedule, which had never fitted comfortably into the regimen of a government office. He arose very early in the morning, sometime between 3:00 and 5:00 A.M., and after a hearty breakfast, began to work. After several hours of writing, he napped to restore his energy. Every few hours of research necessitated a respite in the form of a walk, some shopping, or another nap. Television provided occasional diversion, especially when there was a baseball game to watch, for Jasny was an avid fan. Missing bits of information in his work, or a hunch, frequently sent him to the Library of Congress or to the libraries of the departments of State or Agriculture, where he always felt welcome and where he received much appreciated assistance.

Jasny's study of state and collectivized agriculture was completed in 1948, but even before that he was beginning to turn his attention to the Soviet economy as a whole.

In the section "Detective Work" of the essay "Research on the Soviet Economy" in my Essays on the Soviet Economy (1962), I describe how in 1947 I determined the growth in Soviet industrial output from 1928 to 1937 for "Intricacies of Russian National-Income Indexes" (in Journal of Political Economy). I am very happy that I succeeded in doing it. At that time I was full-time and single-handedly occupied with what turned out to be The Socialized Agriculture, quite a tedious job if one thinks of the thousands (or were there tens of thousands?) of figures, citations, etc. For relaxation I was doing a little of something on the side. Inter alia I was glancing over Y. A. Joffe [I. A. Ioffe], The USSR and the Capitalist Countries, Moscow, 1939. From it I found that there was an earlier edition. A hunch caused me to make the pilgrimage to the U.S. Library of Congress to obtain there Y. A. Joffe, The USSR and the Capitalist World,

Moscow, 1934. A comparison of the two editions at once revealed striking differences. The most conspicuous difference was that according to the earlier edition, the 1928 Soviet industrial production was equal to 10.5 percent of that of the U.S.A., while according to the later edition, it was only 6.7 percent of it, or 35.2 percent less. Considerations which will not be repeated here led to the assumption, to which I still adhere, that the percentage shown represents the exaggeration of the growth of the Soviet industrial production from 1928 to 1937 in the official statistics.

My greatest difficulties started when in 1948 I decided that research on the Soviet economy as conducted in the U.S.A. was biased in favor of Moscow and that I must turn from agriculture to research on the Soviet economy as a whole (rather a daring undertaking for a man of sixty-five). It was important to publish something in a hurry, even at the risk of great imperfections and minor errors, in view of the mess then published and widely circulated in the Western World (Baykov's book,[7] which accepted as true every Soviet figure, was the standard text in American schools then, and there was a lot of other objectionable stuff published on the Soviet economy as if it were the product of research).

A mass of people had acquired sympathy for the U.S.S.R. simply because it was a "socialist" state. They became sympathetic without any familiarity with what was actually going on in the U.S.S.R. or what the nature of Soviet socialism really was, without having studied anything. The Soviets proclaimed that they had socialism, and this settled the issue. When such admirers came to study the situation, there was a natural tendency on their part to see the things in a favorable light. Too deep a penetration into first Leninism and then Stalinism would have been needed for them to suspect that the official evidence was full of lies, that statistics in particular were vastly exaggerating attainments and concealing negative developments. Such students were too deep in their wrong picture to be affected by an occasional publication presenting a view very different from theirs. Another reason for remaining misled was that the writings of the anti-Soviet authors were frequently biased in the opposite direction.

I do not meet many people. Yet among those I have met, there are people whose minds operated like a steel wall from which anything even in the least favorable to the Soviets bounced back, leaving the wall—the mind—exactly as it was before. Fortunately, this category of writers has never had any influence.

Deep disagreements with the bulk of analysts of the Soviet economy in the U.S.A. became apparent at once when I made my bow with my work on the Soviet economy—small bows beginning about 1946, a big bow with *The Socialized Agriculture of the USSR* in 1949. Familiarity with my previous publications would probably have led to a more cautious approach to my new work. But most of those working on the Soviet economy in the U.S.A. had hardly heard of them. Many, having definitely made up their minds, perhaps did not want to hear. It was much simpler to be satisfied with this reasoning: "He is a contributor to the *Socialist Courier* (*Sotsialisticheskii vestnik*), the journal of the Mensheviks, so he must be a Menshevik himself and therefore biased against the Soviets."[8]

It was only natural that the disagreements revealed themselves with particular strength in the attitudes toward the statistics with which every economist had to deal. A special appendix to the *Review of Economic Statistics* (November, 1947) was devoted to a symposium on Soviet statistics. Harry Schwartz, writing on the same subject in the February, 1948 [p. 38], issue of the same journal, started his contribution: "The symposium in the November 1947 issue of this REVIEW represents a landmark in the scientific study of Soviet economic statistics." A little further down he said: "Explicitly or implicitly, each of the contributors to this symposium has indicated his confidence in the basic honesty of Soviet statistics."

Honesty, basic or other, of Stalin's statistics—this certainly was not the line my thought took. I believed that correct analysis of the Soviet economy starts from a realization that many Soviet statistics, expressed in values, can only be regarded as "a pack of lies."*

Adherence to the idea that Soviet statistics are "basically honest" dominated the field to such an extent that not only was I not invited to participate in the statistical symposium, but when, on my own initiative, I hastily prepared a statement presenting the opposite view, the MS was rejected as biased. In a greatly abbreviated form it was published, but with a long delay and with the comment that it still was not entirely free of bias.† The article is commonly cited as important material on Soviet statistics now. The acceptance of the idea that Soviet statistics are "basically honest" made every correct ap-

---

* *The Soviet Economy during the Plan Era* (Stanford University, Calif.: Stanford University Press, 1951), p. 9.

† "Soviet Statistics," *Review of Economics and Statistics*, vol. 32, no. 1 (February, 1950), pp. 92–99.

praisal of the developments in the U.S.S.R. look biased or at least suspect.

The symposium to which Jasny refers was initiated in 1947 by Seymour E. Harris, editor of the Harvard journal the Review of Economic Statistics. Raising the question of the reliability of Soviet statistics, Harris invited five specialists to express their views on the subject: Colin Clark, Alexander Gerschenkron, Paul A. Baran, Abram Bergson, and Aaron Yugow. Jasny, undoubtedly as well qualified but not as well known at that time, was not included. The resulting contributions were published in the November edition of the journal and were summarized in a brief introduction by Harris. Of the five contributors, Clark, director of the Agricultural Economics Research Institute at Oxford, was the only one to stress specific inconsistencies and inaccuracies of Soviet statistics, clearly suggesting deliberate distortion. The others cautiously questioned the accuracy of Soviet statistics and bemoaned their paucity. Abram Bergson, by then a professor of economics at Columbia and a consultant for the Rand Corporation, agreed that "a heightened caution in the use of Soviet statistics certainly is in order." However, he also stated that he could find "no clear evidence of a deliberate intent to mislead" and suggested that there were "at least two positive reasons to think that the data are not falsified."[9]

This was not Jasny's first acquaintance with Professor Bergson's work, for he had seen an article by Bergson, written in 1942, stressing "trustworthy" Soviet statistics.[10] Furthermore, at the time when Jasny had been refused a job with the OSS, Bergson was already employed by them, and in 1944 he had become Chief of the Russian Economics division.[11]

In summarizing the papers for the symposium, editor Harris concluded that the participants, while stressing caution in interpretation of the statistics, generally agreed that they were not deliberately distorted.[12]

Jasny, believing very much to the contrary, must have been extremely frustrated with the tenor of all the papers except Clark's and further irritated by Harris's summary, which virtually ignored Clark's independent stand. However, fully occupied with his agriculture book, he was not goaded into penning a reply until he received the next issue of the journal (this was the February, 1948, issue, to which he refers above), which carried further comments by Maurice

Dobb and Harry Schwartz about the statistical appraisals. Both writers concurred with the majority opinion that Soviet statistics were not deliberately falsified. Schwartz pointed out minor differences, but he completely ignored Colin Clark's position in maintaining that the contributors had indicated their confidence "in the basic honesty of Soviet statistics."[13] Dobb, on the other hand, sarcastically criticized Clark, who, he said, "undaunted by statistical difficulties, such as admitted lack of data on essential points," was "brave enough to make a new and independent computation."[14] This was the final irritation; Jasny could not permit what he saw as petty haggling over details and sarcastic innuendo to conceal the immense distortion which he believed to be so obvious in Soviet statistics. He fired off a response to the journal. In it he was cautiously critical of the participants, using such terms as "not sufficiently careful" and "ill advised."[15] Of the Dobb-Clark argument he wrote, "Instead of meriting Dobb's remarks, Clark's work is a great achievement in throwing light on a vastly distorted subject."[16] Citing example after example of inconsistency in Soviet statistics, Jasny challenged Gerschenkron, Bergson, and Schwartz to prove him wrong. The article was too much for the Harvard journal, and they returned it to Jasny, as he indicates, with some comment about its being biased. Confident in the quality of his own research, Jasny could conclude only that the Review itself deserved the appellation.

However urgent Jasny may have considered publication of a correct appraisal of Soviet statistics, his productivity was slowed briefly, probably in mid 1948, for the removal of a fibroid kidney. Jasny's family was very worried, fearing that the bleeding which he had experienced for several months prior to the operation might forebode malignancy. Happily, the tumor was benign, and its former host recovered quickly from the surgery. Surrounded in bed by his books and notes, and utilizing a piece of fiberboard as a portable desk top, Jasny mounted his one-man campaign to redirect American research on the Soviet economy.

Agriculture is an inseparable part of the whole economy. So a clear picture of the situation in agriculture prevented me from committing big errors in dealing with living standards, real wages, industrial output (at least of consumer goods), etc. These data, together with the estimate of the growth in industrial output in 1928–1937 (discussed above), the fully reliable official data on nonfarm labor, transport (what was transported was also produced), and similar other evidence made it possible to form a correct idea, crude though it might be, of the development of the whole Soviet economy in the period concerned.

Assuming that the results of successive Five-Year Plans (since the first in 1928) "would find their most summary expression in statistics of Soviet national income, if those statistics were available in such form that their validity could be accepted—as they are not,"[17] Jasny set about attempting to produce his own estimates of Soviet national income and its major components:

> Two types of prices were needed for the analysis, whole-sale prices of all goods but particularly of producers' goods, and retail prices of consumers' goods. The latter are needed to deflate nominal wages, which are part of national income. But the other portions of national income, the vitally important industrial production and many other things, cannot be understood without familiarity with the wholesale prices of all major goods.
>
> The retail prices were no problem. They were to be found in the publications of S. N. Prokopovicz, in *Monthly Labor Review*, and in other non-Soviet sources. All that was needed was to combine them into an index. It was different with wholesale prices. For years it was commonly assumed outside Russia that these prices were unobtainable. But research consists to a large extent in not going on assumptions. A more thorough search of the catalogues and stacks of the US Library of Congress brought a little: the Library of the US Dept. of State yielded a rich catch.[18]

In 1949, while Jasny was engaged in his study of national income, his 837-page volume The Socialized Agriculture of the USSR: Plans and Performance, which was published by Stanford University Press, made its appearance. Confident of the impact which his book would have on the study of Soviet statistics, and perhaps somewhat carried away by his cause célèbre, Jasny challenged another periodical for giving too much credence to Soviet figures, this time the highly respected London journal the Economist, which over the past year had published several articles which Jasny believed to have been too generous to the Soviets. A letter from him based on his very negative interpretation of the articles in question was published in the December 31, 1949, issue along with the editor's reply, which slapped Jasny down with "anybody who takes the trouble to re-read the criticised articles will find out how dishonest and ludicrous is the suggestion that they were based on an uncritical acceptance of Soviet statistics."[19]

The sting inflicted by the editor of the Economist must have been assuaged somewhat by scholarly response to Jasny's new book, The Socialized Agriculture. Almost overnight it became an important source for specialists in the Soviet economy as well as the bible for students of Soviet agriculture, and Jasny's name leaped to the top of the list of scholars in the field. The January, 1950, issue of Current History carried a review by N. S. Timosheff, volunteering the extraordinary conclusion: "Nobody will ever be able to add anything of importance to the masterful picture offered by Mr. Jasny."[20] Fifteen years later Colin Clark was to write of Socialized Agriculture:

> This book, I think, was one of the most important of our generation. There had been a number of books, good, bad, and indifferent on Soviet industry; but most of the available books on Soviet agriculture up to that date had been almost fictional in nature.
>
> Some of the writings of the best known western journalists of that time on what was happening in the Russian countryside were pure fiction.[21]

Even those who believed Soviet statistics to be basically reliable could not help being impressed by the scope and depth of Jasny's work. Nor did Jasny's book go unnoticed in Moscow. The November 25 issue of Izvestia carried an objurgatory review which must have given Jasny some satisfaction, if for no other reason, because of its intensity. Furthermore, the editors of the Review of Economics and Statistics now agreed to publish a revised version of Jasny's article which they had rejected in 1948. They did so in their February, 1950, issue.

Early that same month Jasny presented a paper on Soviet prices for a symposium held by the Committee on International Relations at Notre Dame University.[22] In this paper he was critical of contemporary research on the Soviet economy, mentioning specifically Abram Bergson and, by implication, the Rand Corporation and its various consultants in Soviet economics, most of whom Jasny believed accepted Soviet statistics at face value or with little qualification.

The March, 1950, issue of the American Economic Review carried a review of Jasny's The Socialized Agriculture, written by Joseph

A. Kershaw, one of the Rand Corporation's consultants. Although highly appreciative of Jasny's efforts and vigorously applauding the amount and development of his data, Kershaw devoted several pages to criticizing Jasny's interpretations, concluding optimistically that some time that year the labor problems in Soviet agriculture should be well on their way toward solution and that the welfare of the peasant was not an "adequate criterion" by which to judge the success or failure of the socialization of agriculture.[23] His first conclusion probably seemed to Jasny impossibly naïve, and the second, downright cold-blooded.

The tables were turned, however, in December of that year, when Jasny served as a discussant at the annual meeting of the American Economic Association, and one of the papers he agreed to criticize was "The Economic War Potential of the USSR," which was presented by the same J. A. Kershaw.

I opposed with great energy Kershaw's assertion that "the distribution of the national income in the Soviet Union between the consumption and all other sectors is not unlike that in the United States," which implied a huge underestimate of Soviet military expenditures and was equivalent to insisting that there was nothing to worry about in the United States. With reference to the U.S.S.R., I argued [p. 487], "So far as the labor is not employed in the lavish output of munitions and niggardly output of consumers' goods, it is used to produce and transport coal and steel for the munitions, to construct the mines and blast furnaces for the output, and so forth." Professor Edward Ames, who likewise attacked Kershaw at the meeting, shares in the credit due for the correct appraisal of the Soviet military potential at a time when research on the Soviet economy in the U.S.A. was in its baby shoes.

Between Jasny and Ames, Kershaw's major thesis was politely, but thoroughly, demolished. They left untouched, however, Kershaw's peripheral prediction that in the event of an extended cold war, the United States would suffer a seriously disrupting inflation.[24]

The year 1951 also marked the beginning of Jasny's friendship with the editors of Soviet Studies, a quarterly published by the University of Glasgow in Scotland.

Early in 1951 the mail brought proofs of "Problems of Peasant Kolkhoz Organization," intended to be published in a forthcoming issue of Soviet Studies, by Dr. Rudolf Schlesinger, one of the two editors of the journal (it was published in the April, 1951, issue). The proofs were accompanied by a letter challenging me to write a criticism of the lengthy article and guaranteeing that not a word would be changed. Dr. Schlesinger was quite enthusiastic towards the collective-farm system. My negative attitude to it was known from *The Socialized Agriculture*, published one and a half years earlier. My reply to the Schlesinger article carried the unmistakable title "Kolkhozy, the Achilles' Heel of the Soviet Regime" (*Soviet Studies*, October, 1951). Dr. Schlesinger then published an even longer reply, but not without offering me space for a further reply (in both cases without any limitations on the size of my contributions). I actually wrote the reply, but not being satisfied with it, I did not send it in. Repeatedly and fundamentally revised, it forms one of the essays in *Essays on the Soviet Economy*, published ten years later. The behavior of Dr. Schlesinger in the described incident alerted me to the fact that the conducting of journals is quite different in Britain from that in the U.S.A., where such offers as those of Dr. Schlesinger seemed impossible on the basis of my experience. After 1951 I contributed to *Soviet Studies* on very rare occasions until I got a letter from Mr. Jack Miller, the coeditor of the journal, stating that he had discussed the matter with Dr. Schlesinger and they had decided to ask me to become a permanent contributor.

In late 1951 and early 1952 the Food Research Institute, with financial assistance from the Rockefeller Foundation, published the results of Jasny's work on Soviet prices and national income in a series of three monographs, which are referred to in his memoirs as the Triplet: The Soviet Economy during the Plan Era, The Soviet Price System, and Soviet Prices of Producers' Goods. In the first of these volumes, Jasny included a politely critical analysis of Paul A. Baran's computation of Soviet gross national product and national income,[25] a sarcastic reference to Kershaw's review of The Socialized Agriculture,[26] and several critical comments about Abram Bergson's research. Calling one of Bergson's procedures "unquestionably incorrect," Jasny took him to task for qualifying some of his findings in a footnote, "hardly a sufficiently conspicuous place."[27] Jasny followed with a "famous old Russian joke," which he deftly applied to research as he saw it in the Soviet field:

> "If it is written on the cage, 'this is a lion,' but you see
> an ass in the cage, do not trust your eyes." On the iron

curtain is written, "greatly increased consumption levels," "happy, well-to-do life has come to the poverty-stricken Russian worker and peasant," and so on. Through even the tiniest holes in the curtain are clearly discernible the greatly reduced housing space in cities, the diminished supplies of formerly available animal products, the considerably lowered supplies of textiles and many other vital things per capita of both the rural and the urban population. But many students of the Soviet economy stare at the inscription on the cage and refuse to trust their eyes.[28]

Whether Jasny meant to needle Bergson or merely to preview his next volume is not clear, but in a lengthy footnote he promised that in The Soviet Price System, soon to be off the press, he would show "that the procedure used by Bergson in determining the income of the peasants in kind could have yielded a correct result only by happy accident."[29]

Someone's curiosity certainly was aroused:

After publication of the first of the "triplet" . . . , Rand became so anxious to see the sequences that it asked for and obtained from my Institute the proofs on the ground that they were "needed for defence." Now Rand was in an extreme hurry to get at those books [sources discovered by Jasny containing listings of Soviet wholesale prices] in the Library of the US Dept. of State. They were told that I was using the books and that the quickest way would be for the Library to call me up, and a Rand messenger to pick them up at my home and then to return them to me after they had been photostated. This was done by Rand with alacrity.[30]

Volume two of the Triplet became available in November, 1951. True to his word, Jasny had devoted considerable space to criticizing Professor Bergson's methods, beginning on page 3, where the professor's work was cited as an example of "steering in the dark without instruments." Seizing on Bergson's statement that "1937 was for the Soviet consumer a year of unexampled prosperity,"[31] Jasny disproved the contention and castigated the professor for neither checking his data with "other available material" nor drawing the correct conclusions from his inquiry.[32] Although he also faulted Paul Baran, Alexander Baykov, and Maurice Dobb, his harshest criticism was reserved for Bergson, including the vague insinuation: "One wonders what connection exists between Bergson's findings with reference to changes in incomes from 1928 to 1937 and his manner of treating Soviet institutions, which might have been in order in wartime, but seems out of place in 1950."[33] Jasny followed this bit of innuendo with two examples of Bergson's cautious statements which obviously had irritated him.

The third volume of the Triplet, Soviet Prices of Producers' Goods, contains only one brief criticism aimed at Bergson and the mention of an error in Baykov's translation, accompanied by a wry comment.

Although harsh towards those he considered mistaken, Jasny was quick to give credit where he felt credit was due. All three monographs contain repeated compliments to researchers whose work Jasny regarded as useful as well as to those who had helped Jasny with his project. Unfortunately, in his determination to rectify the errors of others, he sometimes went so far, in private conversation and correspondence, as to apply the labels "friends of Moscow" and "fellow travelers" to those whom he considered to be insufficiently negative toward the Soviets. These were terms which did not sit well on the shoulders of serious scholars, however mistaken they might be, especially during the Joseph McCarthy era. Bergson himself has made this point (Bergson to the Lairds, September 8, 1972).

In May, 1952, the Joint Committee on Slavic Studies of the American Council on Learned Societies and the Social Science Research Council sponsored a conference on "Soviet Economic Growth" at Arden House in Harriman, New York, with the goal of forecasting Soviet growth over the next eighteen years, that is, till 1970. The conference was organized and chaired by Professor Bergson, who later combined the papers and commentaries into his book Soviet Economic Growth. At least nine of the participants were Rand consultants. Jasny, too, received an invitation; however, objecting to what seemed to him clearly the intended domination of the conference by the Rand Corporation, he replied by making a "demand for a neutral (non-Rand) chairman."[34] His demand being rejected, Jasny refused to participate in the conference. However, judging from Bergson's book, Jasny was there in spirit, if not in body, for his name and findings are cited more frequently than those of any scholar in the symposium.

HARD TIMES

In mid 1952 the Rockefeller grant which had supported Jasny's research for four years came to an end. At the same time, he and the Food Research Institute at Stanford University terminated their agreement, since his research was by then in general Soviet economic studies rather than in agriculture specifically.[35] This left Jasny with no funds for research and very little to live on. Repeated applications to foundations for assistance produced no positive results. Indeed, some people saw evidence suggesting that Jasny's proposals were being rejected because of his attitude towards Bergson's chairing of the Arden House conference. That incident, apparently, had been inflated all out of proportion, and, along with other misinformation, was being bandied about Harvard-Yale circles as evidence of Jasny's "personal sniping."[36] Jasny, upon learning of the rumors, believed that they were part of a deliberate effort to stifle his research.[37] He registered his frustration and anger by rejecting another invitation, this time to speak on the reliability of Soviet agricultural statistics at the December meeting of the American Statistical Association. Bergson lectured on Soviet statistics in general.

Meanwhile, however, Jasny had acquired copies of the papers presented at the Arden House conference, and taking time out from a new book, one on Soviet industrialization, he prepared his own forecast of Soviet growth, incorporating into it a critical analysis of the papers. The resulting article was published eventually in Social Research (see below).

By spring 1953 the Rand research team apparently had decided to fight fire with fire.
The Triplet got attention, and how. On April, 1953, the *Journal of Political Economy*, published by Chicago University, bestowed the honor of first place on an article "Arithmancy, Theomancy, and Research in the Soviet Economy," by Norman M. Kaplan of Rand Corporation of the Air Force. "Arithmancy and Theomancy" was the research on the Soviet economy by me. In my opinion the vicious attack should not have been printed without having been shown to me sufficiently in advance, and I was not given a fair chance to reply. There is a chain starting from my "Intricacies" (no. 1 in the list of articles below) through my discussion of Kershaw's paper (no. 3 in the same list), my report at Notre Dame early in 1950 (published in *The Soviet Union*, ed. W. Gurian, Notre Dame, 1951), the Triplet,

"Zuwachsraten" (see below) to *Soviet Industrialization, 1928–1952*. Each one is as much arithmancy and theomancy as the other. All of them are the work of a man who found a way to handle Soviet material, and does this whether Moscow or Washington, D.C., likes it or not. What in 1953 could have been presented in a prominent American journal as "Arithmancy and Theomancy" is now generally accepted as good research.

Kaplan's article in the Journal of Political Economy was a scathing criticism of Jasny's research as represented in the Triplet, concluding with this comment: "It is impossible to close without expressing regret for the absence of a judicious editorial blue pencil. The trilogy contains a number of gratuities, personal and political, which are certainly inappropriate in a scientific work, and some of which are defamatory."[38] Jasny submitted a reply to "Arithmancy and Theomancy" entitled "On the Wrong Track," but the editors returned it, suggesting that he remove the "bias." This rejection further convinced Jasny that the "powerful" Rand Corporation "largely controls official research on the Soviet economy . . . also the professional press of the United States with respect to this subject."[39]

One particular characteristic of the work of Bergson and the Rand associates irritated Jasny: that was the use of calculator statistics computed to several decimal places. Jasny, of course, had only a slide rule and a pencil with which to make his rather rough calculations; furthermore, he had no secretaries or research assistants. Rand, on the other hand, could afford to provide its researchers with electronic equipment as well as necessary staff assistance. Jasny argued that, given the Soviets' distorted and limited statistics to begin with, such minutiae as three decimal places were ridiculous. In discussing "Arithmancy, Theomancy . . . " in a footnote to "On the Wrong Track," Jasny grumbled: " 'Arithmancy, Theomancy, etc.' puts up such high requirements for research on the Soviet economy with reference to detail and documentation as can be met only by organizations with hundreds of thousands in funds."[40] Jasny's major objection to Rand, however, was that from his viewpoint its work did not meet the high requirements for research which he put up, namely, "the permanent, honest, and ruthless fight for the truth, for overcoming the bias in oneself, that is indispensable for good results."[41]

The Rand scholars were not alone in the counterattack. In the winter 1953 issue of the Marxist publication Science and Society, *Maurice Dobb of Cambridge University reviewed Jasny's* The Soviet Price System *in vehement and vivid language, far more caustic than any of Jasny's published writings. At one point Dobb criticizes Jasny's "propaganda technique" as "openly polemical—almost monotonously so," but then reverses himself by referring to "this agile propaganda piece."[42] One is surprised at the gentleness with which Jasny treats Dobb's review in his memoirs.*

Dobb wrote: "The picture he [Jasny] paints is not just black in parts, it is uniformly black, black to a degree which strains belief." I am a failure even as a "propagandist," the book is a product of the "cold war," and the reader is "dazed" by me, and so on over six pages in Science and Society, New York, Winter 1953, pp. 83–88.

Dobb was so angry because what I wrote in The Soviet Price System and generally in the "Triplet" was new at that time. Russian research has improved greatly since 1953. Now Professor Dobb would have to condemn every book published on the Soviet economy in recent years. Incidentally the fury of the Cambridge economist is a good testimony to how very urgent it was that the "Triplet" be published in a hurry, even at the risk of great shortcomings and minor errors.

The spring 1954 issue of Social Research *carried a much abbreviated version of Jasny's analysis of the papers given at the Arden House Conference and his own growth forecast. Giving the article the conference title "Soviet Economic Growth," Jasny commended most of the papers and the research in general and was critical of Bergson only briefly, reminding him, in a footnote, that he had labeled 1937 as a year of "unexampled prosperity" for the Soviet consumer.[43] One paper, that of Norman Kaplan, he refused to comment on, "since any criticism of Dr. Kaplan's paper in the Symposium might be interpreted as affected by his share in Rand P-332 ["Arithmancy, Theomancy . . . "]."[44]*

In retrospect, with one or two exceptions, I did not fare badly with my forecasts, which all along the line were higher, some of them much higher, than those made at Arden. As annual rates I had: 7 to 7.5 percent for national income, 9 percent for gross industrial production, 4 to 5 percent for labor productivity in industry, 8 to 9 percent for freight traffic (in ton/kilometers), 9 percent for investment, and 5.5 to 6 percent for private consumption.

The only official index which can be used without any adjustments is that for transport, which shows a rise from 1953 to 1960 of 9 percent per year on the average. The other official indices need some scaling down, and after such treatment they do not differ significantly from my forecasts. As they stand, the official indices, for example, for national income, industry, and labor productivity in industry indicate average annual rises of about 10, 11, and somewhat over 6 percent respectively.

But for gross agricultural output I had only a rate of 3 to 3.5 percent per year (3.5 to 4 percent for net agricultural production). The forecasted rate of growth of labor productivity in agriculture was the same as that for gross agricultural production. The official estimate of somewhat more than 6 percent per year for the growth in gross agricultural production in 1953–1960 is likely to be exaggerated. Still, even the difference between say 5 to 5.5 percent—the probably real rate of growth in gross agricultural production (the rate is something smaller if instead of the period, 1953–1962 is taken)—and my estimate of 3 to 3.5 percent is sufficient for me to feel unhappy. "Soviet Economic Growth" was concluded in July, 1953 (see postscript to the article), too close to Stalin's death to appraise correctly all the repercussions of the event. But this would have been a good reason to postpone publication. The more I study, the more I know, the more averse I become to forecasting. Even the appraisal of the existing situation is difficult enough.

Twenty-one years and a world war after Naum Jasny had left European shores, he returned. In the spring of 1954, Colin Clark, who had met Jasny first in 1947, although he had known his writings for over twenty-five years,[45] invited him to lecture for the Trinity term (April–June), on Soviet agriculture and planning, at the Agricultural Economics Research Institute in Oxford. Having directed his interests toward the Soviet economy as a whole since 1947, Jasny had begun in 1951 to compile the results of his research into a new book on Soviet industrialization. This project he took with him to Oxford. At the end of the term, in early July, Jasny traveled to Göttingen, Germany, to visit his old friend Dr. Arthur Hanau, and to Munich, where he presented a paper in Russian at the Fourth Conference on the Study of the History and Culture of the U.S.S.R.

In the talk I gave at the Russian Institute in Munich, all I was driving at was the platitude "research is search for the truth." No success whatsoever. My methods were too complicated was one of the objections. They were happy when I left.

Meanwhile, the U.S.S.R., under Khrushchev, had begun to publish revised harvest figures for the Stalin years, which proved Jasny's bleak estimates, if anything, somewhat generous. Alec Nove, in his introduction to Soviet Planning, comments: "Unless Khrushchev's statisticians borrowed the 1937 revised harvest figure from Jasny, he [Jasny] must take the credit for having calculated it to within 1 percent."[46] Jasny was delighted. It would be difficult for his detractors to condemn success.

Probably feeling somewhat magnanimous over his victory, Jasny revised his article "On the Wrong Track," taking upon himself the task of pointing out to the Rand Corporation in general and to specific Rand consultants just where they had made their errors in working with Soviet statistics. Although generally polite, Jasny again reminded Bergson of his unfortunate phrase "unexampled prosperity" and seriously set about "correcting" Bergson's calculations. Although the article, which was published in the July, 1956, issue of Soviet Studies, could hardly be called vicious, it certainly must have rubbed salt in wounds perhaps already irritated by Soviet confirmation of Jasny's estimates. At least one member of the Rand research team could not let the article go unanswered, for the next issue of Soviet Studies carried a letter written under the Rand letterhead by Oleg Hoeffding of the Economics Division, castigating Jasny for his "vitriolic" and "intemperate attacks" on Rand researchers.[47] Determined to have the last word, Jasny fired off a reply to Hoeffding's letter, which Soviet Studies printed with the obvious intention that it should, indeed, be the last. The following comment preceded the letter: "In publishing the following reply by Dr. Jasny to Mr. Hoeffding's letter in the last issue of Soviet Studies, the editors close the discussion so far as personal aspects and imputations of motive are concerned. They hope, however, that discussion will continue on the important questions of fact and method in work upon the Soviet economy which underlie this controversy."[48] In his letter, Jasny effectively refuted some of Hoeffding's points, misinterpreted others, and undoubtedly believed in his own innocence when he berated Hoeffding for having attacked "one whose only fault was to have pointed out the shortcomings."[49]

"BIAS"

Having pinned the label "biased" on opponents, as well as having smarted under the accusation himself, Jasny examined the subject at some length in his autobiography.

Bias is by no means restricted to research on the Soviet economy. It is indeed quite a widespread weakness in research. It is individual mostly. A scholar builds up an opinion on the basis of his good or not so good research, and once the opinion is formed, he sticks to it, although repeated and more penetrating analysis would have led to modification or abandonment of the original idea. One must keep one's mind permanently open and not be too sure of any finding. One must be prepared to change or at least reconsider on the slightest provocation, etc.

When, in working on the grains in classical antiquity, I discovered that the role of wheat in antiquity, relative to that of barley, had been greatly exaggerated in the historical literature, the chance of correcting an error in historical science of possibly hundreds of years' duration so excited me temporarily that I had to suppress an urge to make barley even more important than could be justified by the evidence. I hope I was successful, but one never can be certain in such things.

But bias may also be collective. Historical work has for a long time been showing a strongly pronounced tendency to ameliorate the past, to place phenomena hundreds of years before their real time. I got specific credit for a realistic approach to the past. But all the bias which can be found in scholarly work is almost nothing as compared with the immense amount of it which has prevailed in research on the Soviet economy.

Contrary to most others in the field, I, as already mentioned, turned to work on the Soviet economy in earnest only after about thirty years of research in other fields. This research had in general met with some approval. Apart from other reasons, I had enough ambition to do everything in my power not to permit my research to deteriorate when I turned, full scale, first to Soviet agriculture and then to the Soviet economy as a whole. Bias would obviously have caused a great deterioration.

The very fact that my work on the Soviet economy was widely considered biased made advisable special efforts to avoid any error to the detriment of the Bolsheviks. I also realized the danger that my dislike of the dictatorship might subconsciously operate in the direction of presenting too dark a picture. The danger was counteracted by deliberately giving the benefit of doubt to the Soviets.*

Absence of statistical help has compelled me to abstain from analyses which I otherwise would have done. It has forced me to use official data to a larger extent and with fewer adjustments than was good for the correctness of my results. Here is another reason for my presentation leaning to the more favorable side for the Soviets. My estimate of a 65 percent growth in industrial output in 1950–1955 was largely a scaling down of the official figure for it of 85 percent for the obvious exaggeration in the growth of the machinery output, leaving untouched the likely exaggeration in some other items. Yet an increase in industrial output of 65 percent in five years—which included such growth-disturbing factors as the switch on a large scale to armament production during the Korean War,† and the shift to consumer goods after Stalin's death in 1953—seems excessive.

Let Gardner Clark of Cornell speak of the fate of *The Socialized Agriculture of the USSR*, Stanford, 1949: "A decade ago his [Jasny's] critical appraisal of Soviet agriculture was generally considered to be prejudiced and extreme. Then starting in 1953, Khrushchev came out with a series of blasts that turned Jasny's extreme strictures into understatements."‡

---

* Here, too, an error is frequently committed in believing me an enemy of everything going on in the U.S.S.R. This is true only if all that is going on in the U.S.S.R. is believed to be limited to dictatorship. I certainly am not an enemy of socialism, state ownership of means of production, planning, socialized medicine, and many other things. What I am definitely against is dictatorship, coercion in all its forms, absence of freedom, indeed slavery in many respects. I need freedom, first of all, for myself. I cannot do without it. But I believe freedom a good thing also for everybody else, not only for Americans, but for Russians as well, as a basis of the organization of social life. This attitude toward freedom should not cause any difficulties in the U.S.A., but it does.

† Some analysts explain the near stagnation in industrial growth during the Purge Era (1936–1940) fully by preparations for war. If this effect were so strong, it would have operated with considerable force also during the Korean War. It would help analysis if much less significance were assigned to war preparations as a growth-retarding factor during the Purge Era and if some importance were assigned to the same factor in the period during the Korean War.

‡ Review of *Soviet Industrialization, 1928–1952* in the *Russian Review*, vol. 21, no. 2 (April, 1962), p. 190.

I certainly was pleased to read Clark's statement which preceded that cited: "Jasny has a knack in getting authoritative support for his point of view."

Discussing in "Jasny's 'Agriculture' Revisited" ('Agriculture' stands for *The Socialized Agriculture of the USSR*) my estimates of the grain output of the U.S.S.R. in the 1930s, Alec Nove said: "Where he is wrong, he errs on the side of *insufficiently* allowing for official exaggerations."* This remark applies also to most other of my estimates. If one takes the trouble to compare my estimates with those of other Western scholars or with official evidence, after these were corrected years later, my estimates are mostly higher—not much higher, but higher.

One of the factors which made my estimates of gross agricultural production in the 1930s tend to be somewhat too high was that I failed to detect that in complete secrecy the "biological yield" (the instrument of greatly exaggerating yields) was applied not only to grain (this was announced officially and corrected by me), but also to potatoes, sunflower seed, and flax. Fortunately, these crops are of secondary importance.

As recently as 1961 and 1962, when the evidence, previously concealed, concerning the production costs of animal products to the collective farms was ultimately disclosed, these costs turned out to be much higher than I had thought. This implied a much greater inefficiency of the "socialist" form of farm organization than had seemed possible. Fortunately, I did not publish anything on this topic before disclosure of this evidence.

The question of who was biased is reflected in the attitude of the various students toward their earlier publications. Bergson wants his "unexampled prosperity," cited below, to be forgotten. So does Schwartz with reference to his "basic honesty." There is no need for me to want any of my major statements erased from memory.

There were, it is true, some difficulties in classing me as biased against the Soviets. In 1951 I published a study on concentration-camp labor.† While the commonly circulated estimates of the number of inmates in the camps were 10 and more millions, even 18

---

* *Soviet Studies*, vol. 12, no. 2 (October, 1960), p. 191.

† "Labor and Output in Soviet Concentration Camps," *Journal of Political Economy* vol. 59, no. 5 (October, 1951), pp. 405–19.

millions,* my estimate (for 1941) was only 3.5 million. It was reported to me that the New York anti-Soviets classed me as pro-Soviet for this piece of research. If the pro-Soviets accepted my calculations as proof of absence of bias, this has remained unknown to me. It is, incidentally, interesting that I made the study of concentration-camp labor at the request of the union of former concentration-camp inmates and specifically on the suggestion of the late David Dallin, who was responsible for one of the high estimates.[50] They persisted in their request after I had warned them that my estimate of the number of inmates was very low (I certainly was not anxious to handle this hot potato). This and other less-prominent proofs of absence of bias were successfully overlooked.

It is more than natural that in the U.S.S.R. they are not enthusiastic about my writings. With an eye on my "Plan and Superplan," S. Khavina called me in a journal of the All-Union Academy of Sciences†—in a rather unladylike manner—"an 'expert' in anticommunism and falsification of evidence on the development of the Soviet economy." This was only the last in a rather long line of similar compliments bestowed upon me from time to time. But who does not know that they *have* to write in this way? For a considerable time now I have felt that they are impressed in Russia by my writings. Indeed, being dependent on their grain crop for their daily bread, they may be impressed even more than the West at the fact that as early as 1949 I succeeded in scaling down correctly the official biological grain yields in the U.S.S.R. for the years from way back in 1928 (when the official revisions were published in 1958, they turned out to be practically identical with mine). It may be self-indulgence, but I think that there are quite a few scholars in Russia who know that my research is honest, that it is as true as it can be from 8,000 miles away, with all the concealments and distortions in the official data and the difficulties encountered in the U.S.A. An American scholar during his recent stay in Moscow was asked about my activities by some Soviet economists. He sums up his impressions of a rather lengthy discussion as follows: "They resent what Jasny writes, but they are proud that it is written by a Russian." Not bad, not bad at all.

To conclude this section on bias, let me quote the development

* United Nations, *Ad-Hoc Committee on Forced Labor Report*, Geneva, 1953.

† *Questions of Economics*, July, 1962, p. 99.

in the appraisal of real wages during the crucial period from 1928 to 1937. In 1950 Professor Bergson wrote: "1937 was for the Soviet consumer a year of unexampled prosperity."* In December of the same year, at the meeting of the American Economic Association, I presented a calculation according to which nominal wages had increased in 1928–1937 by 332 percent, while living costs had risen by 600 percent during the same period,† implying a real wage in 1937 of only 61.7 percent of that of 1928. At the end of 1951, in *The Soviet Economy during the Plan Era*, Stanford, 1951, p. 69, I reduced the estimate of the 1937 real wage in terms of 1928 moderately from 61.7 to 57.6 percent. In his book *Soviet National Income and Product in 1937*, 1953, p. 10, Professor Bergson repeated a statement from his 1950 article mentioned above: "Living standards in 1937 probably were higher than in any year since 1928, . . . and according to some indications may even have surpassed those of the earlier year." In 1954 Mrs. Janet Chapman, a Bergson pupil, estimated the real wage of nonfarm workers in 1937 in 1928 weights at 58% of those in 1928, but at 82% in 1937 weights.‡

In 1961, Bergson reproduced and accepted the estimate of real wages of nonfarm workers in 1937 made by Mrs. Janet Chapman of 55.6 percent of those in 1928 "in prevailing prices of 1937."§ Thus it took the Bergson group exactly ten years to reach an estimate practically identical with mine made in 1951.

I do not need to emphasize that a correct appraisal of the development of the Soviet economy in the vastly important period from 1928 to 1937 is impossible without a correct calculation of the development in real wages during that period.

The idea that I was biased ultimately weakened greatly or completely disappeared. The bias that does dominate me in the final analysis is the one against falseness.

Endowed as he was with a "crusading spirit,"[51] Jasny possessed the personal discipline and enthusiasm to reach his peak of productivity during his free-lance period. From 1954 to 1956 alone, for

---

* "Soviet National Income and Product in 1937," *Quarterly Journal of Economics*, vol. 64, no. 3 (August, 1950), p. 423.

† "Papers and Proceedings," *American Economic Review*, vol. 41, no. 2 (May, 1951), p. 488.

‡ *Review of Economics and Statistics*, May, 1954.

§ *The Real National Income of Soviet Russia since 1928* (Cambridge, Mass.: Harvard University Press, 1961), p. 256.

example, he turned out some seventeen articles and one monograph and completed the first draft of his next book. Unfortunately, however, he was unable to find enough American outlets, especially in professional journals, for all of his articles, and he became increasingly frustrated in his dealings with American editors and publishers.

I had great difficulties in publishing my material. Refusals to accept, anonymous editorial readers not rarely incompetent, editors frequently ignorant and on occasion biased, delays in publishing lasting years—I had an ample fill of all this.

Between 1954 and 1962 I did not publish anything in an American professional journal. Why subject myself to the risk of negative answers (they make me very unhappy), to suggestions to submit for examination (I shudder only to think of the phrase), to dealing with not-so-good editors, fellow travelers as editorial readers, protected by anonymity,* etc., when the return of the air mail brings from London, Glasgow, or several other places in Germany, France, or Italy the message that the journal would be pleased, some even say "delighted," to publish my contribution.

The difficulties I experienced in publishing in the U.S.A. have, in the last analysis, been to the good. They encouraged me to turn to European outlets.

In 1955 Jasny completed the first "final" draft of his new book Soviet Industrialization, 1928–1952. *Although it contained fewer pages (467) than his* The Socialized Agriculture of the USSR, *this book, focussing on "Stalin's great drive for industrialization," would vie with the earlier one in importance.*

One of the issues dealt with in my article "Soviet Economic Growth" [see above] was periodization, which I later developed in *Soviet Industrialization*. I threw overboard the periodization by five-year-plan periods used in the U.S.S.R. and slavishly followed in the West, because it lacked economic significance and indeed largely represented misleading propaganda.

Sometimes the ways of analysis appear too complicated, and I give up the problem entirely. This is, for example, one of the reasons why my periodization of the Stalin era of industrialization does not

---

* The anonymity is actually one-sided. If the comment is unfavorable, the reviewer keeps silent. When it is favorable, the reviewer sometimes finds an occasion to notify the author of his role, possibly to put him under a kind of obligation.

contain a period for World War II. For my way of analysis, at least a vague idea of the changes from year to year were needed, not just a jump from 1940 to 1945, as is usually done. But this seemed to require more time than I was inclined to spend. All I succeeded in doing with reference to the period of World War II was an analysis of the prices and the quantities turned over in kolkhoz markets, year by year. There seemed too little material on the war period to make a chapter of it. So I included it in the section dealing with the period "Stalin Has Everything His Way," and this met with an energetic disapproval by Gardner Clark in his review of my book.*

My periodization now seems on the way to more or less general acceptance, showing that one has to operate with an ax rather than a small knife.

Penning in his last corrections, Jasny sent his book to Colin Clark's institute at Oxford, where it was edited by Hans Frankel and Clark.

In 1956 the Soviet Union published its first Statistical Handbook. Jasny, inspired, immediately set about recalculating the official statistics on the basis of his own research, and presented them with appropriate comments in his The Soviet 1956 Handbook: A Commentary, published in 1957 by the Michigan State University Press. According to the preface, the book "does not attempt to minimize Soviet attainments. Rather, its purpose is to examine the impossibly large rates of growth claimed in official Soviet statistics and to reduce them to their real proportions." This feat evoked the following reaction from Jasny's economist friend Hans Richter: "Nowhere else has Jasny's mastery of Soviet statistics and his deep understanding and 'feel' for practical economic statistics been shown more impressively."[52]

Incorporating in his Soviet Industrialization manuscript some of the suggestions made by Colin Clark's institute, Jasny began what must have seemed an interminable search for a publisher for his new book. Repeated rejections must have strengthened his conviction that his work was being ostracized because of the quarrel with Bergson and the Rand Corporation. In the summer of 1958 he revised the book, bringing it up to date, and sent it to a European publisher who at first reacted favorably to the work. After visiting the United States, notably the West Coast, however, the publisher rejected Jasny's book,

---

* Russian Review, April, 1962, p. 190.

further convincing him of Rand's negative influence.[53] After two further "goings-over," in the summer of 1959 and the spring of 1960, Jasny obtained financial assistance for publication of his work through the Joint Committee on Slavic Studies of the American Council of Learned Societies and the Social Science Research Council, and his book was published by the University of Chicago Press in 1961.

In dedicating the book "to Vladimir Gustavovich Groman, the planner, the fighter, the great man," Jasny partially fulfilled a long-held desire to dedicate "the best writing that I could master,"[54] a monograph on planning, to his former friend and colleague. In the preface he explained, "Since this work is probably one of my last major efforts, it must serve as a substitute." Jasny also gave considerable credit to another friend and colleague when he wrote: "The various phases involved in Soviet postwar agricultural development were almost endlessly talked over with Mrs. Luba Richter of the U.S. State Department, so that it is impossible to keep apart what is hers and what is mine."[55]

The first review appeared in the November issue of Annals of the American Academy of Political and Social Sciences. In it J. S. Prybyla termed the book "a monument to painstaking individual research resting on mature judgment, insight, and a sure grasp of analytical techniques."[56] In the April, 1962, issue of the American Historical Review, David Granick commented, "When one considers that the book was written by a man in his seventies, who had neither clerical aid nor graduate assistants, both its vigor and its breadth of scholarship are quite astonishing."[57] In the September issue of the American Economic Review, Alexander Erlich praised the book as "another important addition," "rich fare," and "Herculean."[58] However, all those who reviewed Soviet Industrialization were critical of what Erlich termed Jasny's "rule of thumb" technique, and although some praised him for thoroughness, others complained of excessive detail. The consensus, however, acknowledged the work as an extraordinary accomplishment for a man in his seventies and as an important source for scholars in the field.

FESTSCHRIFT AND PLAUDITS

For over fifteen years during the 1950s and early 1960s, Naum Jasny's apartment in Naylor Gardens, Washington, D.C., doubled as his office. From there he could easily travel by bus to the Library of Congress or to the State Department or the Agriculture Department to conduct his research and to compare his findings with those of friends and colleagues. Until 1953 his younger daughter, Tanya, and her family—by then including two youngsters, Lynda (1946) and Philip (1948)—lived just around the corner. This proximity yielded its advantages in the form of almost daily family dinners which included Naum, thus ensuring his having a balanced diet and the companionship of his grandchildren, whom he enjoyed immensely. In 1953, however, Tanya's family moved to Silver Spring, thus reducing the frequency of contacts with her father.

Sometime in the late 1950s Tanya noted a sudden drop in her father's weight. Over a period of approximately six weeks he lost some fifteen pounds, leaving his trousers hanging loosely from his belt. Recognizing the loss of weight as a possible danger signal, Tanya called Natascha, who by then was living in Princeton, New Jersey.[59] Somewhat fearful, the daughters determined that their father must have a physical examination immediately, however much he might protest. Natascha was elected to escort him to the doctor's office. In due course, the journey was undertaken and the examination completed, but the doctor could suggest no satisfactory explanation for the loss of weight. Still worried, Natascha called a taxi, and she and Naum started for home. On the way, her father began to recount a magazine article he had read some time before, setting forth the evils of excess cholesterol in the body.

"I have decided," announced Naum, "that I'm not going to use any fat or oil at all any more, and for six weeks I haven't touched a speck of butter."

Natascha exploded, "Pulyinka!" she cried, "Why didn't you tell me that before we went to the doctor?" Preoccupied as he was with his research, the most obvious result of a fat-free diet had never occurred to Naum.

Sometime in 1960 the Institute for the Study of the U.S.S.R. in Munich agreed to publish four of Jasny's essays on the Soviet economy as a monograph. Will Klump, then working in the New York office with Jaan Pennar, undertook the job of editor, which necessitated frequent communication with Jasny on minor alterations and additions. At one time during the two-year project, Jasny traveled to New York to observe the progress first hand. Pennar and Klump treated him and his old friend George Denike to pelmeny (meat dumplings) at a Russian tearoom and were surprised to discover that they could not compete with the old gentlemen when it came to consuming vodka.[60]

Recalling with pleasure his previous sojourns in Europe, Jasny eagerly anticipated another visit. In 1961, circumstances developed which made a return trip possible. In the first place, Natascha's husband was on sabbatical leave in Florence, Italy, that year so that Naum could be near a member of his family in case of emergency, and secondly, he had received several invitations to lecture in Europe. Boarding a ship in New York, Jasny sailed for Italy. It was a pleasant journey, made especially delightful by frequent chats with the ice-cream-cone set, whose company he enjoyed so much and whose affections he attracted naturally.

Jasny arrived in Florence in excellent health, although he looked rather bedraggled, since, with his customary lack of regard for his appearance, he had brought with him only one suit, albeit with two pairs of pants. Wanting her father to look reasonably neat and clean for a lecture he was scheduled to give at the Agricultural Institute in Rome, Natascha suggested sending his clothes to the cleaners. Naum, objecting to the cost, refused. Repeated appeals on Natascha's part eventually extracted a concession—she could take the trousers, but no amount of persuasion would part Jasny from his coat. "If I would have always wasted all my money on dry cleaning," he pointed out, "I couldn't have afforded to have Philya in a private hospital." Natascha acquiesced, then spent two hours spot-cleaning and pressing his coat.

Jasny's earlier ingress into antiquity now made it imperative for him to make an excursion to the ruins of ancient Pompeii. Natascha, although fearing that such a tour would be exhausting for a seventy-eight-year-old man, agreed to drive him there. She was delighted, though somewhat embarrassed, to discover that, in fact, her father tired less easily than she. Indeed, Jasny's health was sound enough that he could undertake a rather vigorous travel schedule. Following his lecture in Rome, he journeyed northward through Italy, observing Italian agriculture at first hand and collecting data for yet another book he was contemplating. Arriving in Germany, he delivered a second lecture at the Munich Institute for the Study of the U.S.S.R. and discussed his forthcoming book of essays with editor Will Klump, who also was in Munich by then. Jasny then traveled north to Göttingen, where he again visited his old friend Arthur Hanau. Continuing on to Kiel, he lectured at the Weltwirtschaftliches Institut. His last lecture, apparently, was in London, where, for the first time, he met Jack Miller, editor of Soviet Studies, and Jane Degras, the only female editor he ever liked.[61] Returning to Italy for the remainder of his stay, Jasny boarded a ship at Venice and sailed for New York after some two months' sojourn.[62]

Whether the suggestion was made in person or by letter, we do not know, but it was in 1961 that Jack Miller first broached the subject of memoirs to Jasny. He was intrigued.

The idea for me to write an autobiography is due to Mr. Jack Miller of the University of Glasgow, Scotland, an editor of Soviet Studies, a quarterly published by that university, to which, after a slow start, I have contributed rather profusely in the past few years.

After a rather prolonged period of meditation, I decided that the idea of an autobiography, even if sound at all, could not be implemented in the form of a more or less comprehensive calendar narrative, boring even to think of, but only by handling selected separate periods and even individual incidents which might be of sufficient interest for one reason or another.

Thus rejecting a "calendar narrative," Jasny began putting down on paper some of his recollections, leaving out long periods of his life and activities about which his readers could only speculate. He called his work The Adventures of an Economic Analyst.

Early in 1962 Jasny's book Essays on the Soviet Economy, published jointly by the Munich Institute and Praeger, came off the press. Page v carried what had become Jasny's motto—Luba Richter calls it his "battle cry"—"Through frankly acknowledged errors to the truth!" Furthermore he emphasized the point by once again dredging up Abram Bergson's "unexampled prosperity."[63]

In spite of Jasny's having outwalked Natascha in Pompeii, his health had begun to deteriorate. Rest periods became necessary with increasing frequency, and writing sapped his strength. Often he felt too tired to leave his apartment and was forced to postpone essential reading in the Library of Congress. At other times, however, Jasny experienced partial recovery and found the energy to do the things he wished. It was during one of these periods of improvement in September, 1962, that Jasny flew to Lawrence, Kansas, to present his paper "Low- and High-Yielding Crops in the USSR" at the University of Kansas Conference on Soviet Agricultural and Peasant Affairs (September 20–22, 1962).[64] In this paper, which was the precursor of the book on which he had commenced work (Khrushchev's Crop Policy), Jasny vigorously attacked Khrushchev's "new agronomy," comparing cropping in the U.S.S.R. with that in Western agriculture. Jasny's vigor, however, by then was coming only in short bursts, between which he needed rest. A cot was set up for him in a nearby office of the Student Union, where he could recuperate his strength. Mrs. Richter, who also attended the conference, kept tab on her ailing friend, buffering him from the strain and confusion.

Returning to Washington, Jasny continued work on his latest book. During the increasingly frequent periods of poor health, when he was confined to his apartment, he worked on his autobiography, completing it sometime during 1962 and mailing it to Jack Miller for editing.

Although birthdays traditionally had been important occasions in the Jasny family, Naum's eightieth birthday was especially significant. There were two celebrations. One was a private affair at Tanya's house in Silver Spring, where some thirty or forty family members and close friends listened to George Denike and Hans Richter pay tribute to the grand old patriarch, and watched as his family presented him with a very special gift, a loaf of bread baked in Thebes in about 1400 B.C. and preserved in an Egyptian tomb until it was excavated in 1935. Another gift, one presented to Jasny by the Richters, was a ten-page bibliography of his books and articles.[65] The second celebration honoring his birthday was held near the end of February in the Brookings Institution Building in Washington. Some thirty to forty friends and colleagues honored Jasny at a dinner, which was followed with a highly laudatory speech by Edward Allen. At a separate meeting, the celebration was continued with a paper by Russell Greenslade, paying further tribute to Jasny's contribution to research; one by Luba Richter, complimenting "Jasny, the Man"; and a paraphrase of his earlier eulogy by historian George Denike. Jasny himself spoke briefly and distributed a samokritika ("self-criticism") page entitled "How Stupid Can One Be?" in which he pointed out the inconsistency of the Soviets' official national income index with their index for gross agricultural production, a contradiction which until then had gone unnoticed by Western scholars.[66] The celebration was capped by the arrival of congratulatory letters and telegrams from friends and scholars the world over. Later that year the Munich Institute honored Jasny by printing a brief biography in Russian entitled simply Naum Mikhailovich Jasny. Written by B. G. Armbruster, the information probably was taken in large part from the memoirs manuscript, to which Armbruster had access. Jasny, being unaware of this fact and having never met the author, was surprised at his accuracy, and very much pleased. Furthermore, he hoped that it might be translated into English and German.[67]

In spite of the fact that writing was becoming increasingly difficult for the octogenarian, he set about revising "How Stupid Can One Be?" for publication in Soviet Studies,[68] wrote a second article for that journal, and in November completed his book Khrushchev's Crop Policy. This, too, he sent to Glasgow.

The following year, 1964, Jasny received another plaudit in the form of a book of essays called Soviet Planning: Essays in Honour of Naum Jasny. Edited by Jane Degras and Alec Nove and published by Blackwell, this volume contained papers written by friends and respected colleagues, a brief bibliography, and a short essay by Dr. Hans Richter, "Jasny at Eighty," recounting Jasny's accomplishments and describing succinctly his personality and traits.

Meanwhile, Jasny was putting together his recollections of early associations with a number of important Menshevik and neo-Narodnik economists of the 1920s; this he entitled Names to Be Remembered, and it was soon to follow his memoirs to Europe. A second conference on Soviet agriculture was held in the spring of 1964 at the Munich Institute, to which Jasny was invited. Unfortunately, increasing feebleness prevented his making the long trip. In August of 1965, however, he found the energy to fly to Santa Barbara, California, for the third such conference, for which he was designated Honorary Chairman, and at which he presented a paper entitled "Production Costs and Prices in Soviet Agriculture." A banquet was held in Jasny's honor, with the benign old patriarch reigning supreme at the head table. The conferees paid him homage with eloquent praise, which was modified only slightly by scholarly acknowledgment of his imperfections. Apparently, the underlying melancholy of finality sensed by Jasny's friends and peers had little effect on the man himself, for he returned to Washington, impatient to continue his work.

Jasny's final book, Khrushchev's Crop Policy, finished in 1963, had at last been published by the Institute of Soviet and East European Studies at Glasgow. Unfortunately, during the intervening years, Khrushchev had been removed from power, but the book still was valued by reviewers as a diagnosis of certain illnesses still afflicting the U.S.S.R. and a prescription for improvement (see below).

By early 1966 Jasny's health had degenerated to the degree that writing extracted a tremendous toll. He had suffered a light stroke and was forced to give up his apartment at Naylor Gardens. For a while he stayed with Tanya in Silver Spring, and then, when he was feeling better, he moved into the Roosevelt Hotel, a residential hotel designed to accommodate senior citizens with failing health. There he could stay in bed much of the day, working when he felt like it in a prone position with his piece of fiberboard for a desk, shifting frequently and resting often. On rare occasions he felt up to a brief excursion to the library, but usually his questions had to be answered as well as possible over the telephone. A typist came in to pick up materials to be typed and to deliver the work upon completion. Refusing to give up long after most people would have rested on their laurels, Jasny continued writing. Besides preparing the Santa Barbara paper for publication in a volume (an undertaking which must have cost Jasny dearly, as in a footnote he refers to the work as "torture"),[69] he also turned out a brief review for Soviet Studies on Boris Nikolaevsky's Power and the Soviet Elite. These were to be Jasny's last articles; although in May, in a letter to Jack Miller, he was still hoping to write yet another on national-income statistics, to be entitled "They Call It Statistics." "But," he concluded, "I am afraid my writing is over."

The spring issues of Problems of Communism and Survey came out with very favorable reviews of Khrushchev's Crop Policy. Jasny, who had not anticipated "such high praise," was much pleased with what he referred to as "very pleasant concluding acts."[70] There was, at this time, however, a matter which weighed heavily on his mind; his autobiography had been rejected by several publishers and at that time lay in the hands of Max Hayward of St. Antony's College at Oxford, where it had been for nearly a year. His other manuscript, Names to Be Remembered, was not faring much better. Jasny decided to appeal to Jack Miller, in the hope that he could intercede and expedite the publication of both. Miller immediately set about trying to locate the manuscripts and to ascertain the potential publishers' intentions. Impatience and a sense of urgency filled Jasny's notes inquiring about the manuscripts. At one point, after having heard nothing of the matter for some time, he wrote, "At my age such long waiting seems a luxury."[71]

Sometime in early spring (1966), Jasny learned that he was to receive an honorary degree of Doctor of Agricultural Science from the

Georg-August University of Göttingen, Germany. He was greatly pleased and wrote in one of his short notes to Miller in early September: "I really do not know why all this trouble. There would be more sense if this were done in the U.S.A. or the U.K. I am in any case very proud."[72] On Thursday, September 8, during a solemn ceremony at the German Embassy in Washington, D.C., the appropriate scroll was presented to Jasny by Professor Walter Schaefer-Kehnert, representing the Agricultural Faculty of the university. Dr. Hans Richter delivered the customary laudate, and the ceremony was presided over by the German minister, Baron von Stackelberg. Although many had mistakenly addressed him as Dr. Jasny before, he could now, for the first time, answer to that title without mental reservation.

Somewhat later that month, Jasny received notice from Stanford University Press that in November they would print a second edition of his The Socialized Agriculture of the USSR. He was "pleasantly surprised," as he had assumed for some time that the limited appeal of his subject matter would never justify a second edition of any of his books.[73] He was, however, becoming increasingly disturbed over the lingering fate of his memoirs and of Names to Be Remembered. Reflecting the accelerating deterioration of his health, his letters, while still urgent, took on a plaintive tone. The last of October he wrote to Miller, "I am generally in a state of decomposition and what I write does not matter."[74] On November 18, in response to a letter from Miller, he commented, "Each time when I hear about my biography and the second book, it is as if I am spitted on." Two days later, experiencing some difficulty with the date in the heading of his letter, he wrote, "I am afraid of getting senile, but there is hope that this is premature." Jasny's last letter to Miller was written on November 28, 1966. Although his handwriting was somewhat shaky, the text was entirely coherent, describing the further delay in publication as "very deplorable."

Around the middle of January, Jasny suffered a stroke, which sent him to the hospital in serious condition. In February he was able to return to his apartment, but only under the care of a private nurse. He was by then quite feeble, still recognizing his family and friends, but unable or unwilling to carry on a conversation. A series of strokes followed, alternating with periods of partial recovery. By early April, Jasny had been moved to the Randolph Hills Nursing Home in Wheaton, Maryland, still under the care of the private nurse, whom he had grown to like very much and who could readily divine his needs.[75] In mid April he slipped into a coma, and on April 22, 1967, "he who had been a fighter all his life died peacefully."[76]

8—Jasny: The Man and His Work

UNIVERSALIST

I am sometimes asked what method I follow in my analysis. My answer is: "None, so far as I know." Perhaps it is with me as with Molière's Monsieur Jourdain, who did not realize that all his life he had been talking in prose. I just take the problem in hand, be it wide or narrow, and try to find the answer to it, by ways which seem within my means.

Hunches and similar things play a great role in successful research on the Soviet economy. But such stimuli, if any, were only at the beginning of my analyses. Hunches and the like helped to find that a problem exists. But I did not print just hunches, anything that I did not believe proven by evidence, though the evidence may still have been my own estimates. (Without making his own estimates, any good researcher will find analysis of Soviet economic developments to be impossible.)

An editor suggested that my essay "Research in the Soviet Economy," much later published as one of the *Essays on the Soviet Economy*, should have the phrase "Detective Work" in its title. Research on Soviet Russia actually to a large extent has this character.

Naum Jasny was perhaps at his best doing "detective work" research. His broad range of knowledge and experience, as well as his active imagination, provided the fertile soil from which his hunches sprouted. They also supplied him with a mental plotting board on which he could check and weigh each element in its relation to the total picture, enabling him to avoid the errors committed by many scholars who are restricted by narrower vision. Professor Alec Nove, in his introduction to Soviet Planning, wrote of Jasny: "The breadth of his horizon, the extent of his interests and knowledge, enable him to spot inter-connections or illogicalities which sometimes elude those of us who specialize more narrowly in particular fields. He has an unerring eye for spotting important questions, he selects worthwhile targets for critical analysis."[1] Jasny himself was somewhat modest on the subject.

Sometimes I am given credit for a kind of universalism in my knowledge. Actually I am immensely specialized. I do not follow progress in economic, statistical, or other theory. I do not know what is going on in the economy, not only of the United States or any other capitalist country, but even in those of the satellite countries, familarity with which would be very helpful in answering, amongst many others, such an extremely important question as: What part of the reduction in living standards in the U.S.S.R. was indispensable in the industrialization drive and what was the part which must be charged definitely and specifically against Stalin?

I always devote my full attention to one subject at any given time, but take this subject rather broadly. For more than twenty years it was the economy of the five major grains in the Western world. In one group they even laughed about my "narrowness," in ridicule calling me "The Five Grains." But I simply replaced width with depth. What I did with the subject as I understood it may even be called a widely ramified coverage.

The desire to understand why grains are grown and why one and not the other grain is chosen led me to study climate and soil. I did not become either a climatologist or a soil specialist. Of climate I tried to know the main features of the countries and the parts of the countries I was interested in, insofar as these features affect grain growing (annual, seasonal, and monthly temperatures and precipitations, length of frost-free periods, etc.). The same pertains to soil. I did not pay much attention to why a soil is such and not other, although it is difficult to fail to pick up something, but I concentrated on the effect of the soils as they are on the growth of grain in general and of the various grains in particular.

I felt a certain familiarity with farm techniques to be indispensable, and a little botany promised to clear up many points.

Grain is grown on land which in most cases is used, or can be used, for some other crops. So, one must know a little about these other crops, in the first place oilseeds, sugar beets, etc. But I never knew much about fruit and vegetable growing or, of course, about countries which grew little or no grain.

To know the reasons why grain in general and various grains in particular are grown, one needs, furthermore, to familiarize oneself with how grain in general and the various grains in particular are utilized by man and beasts (for beasts, mainly usefulness; for men, also preference). Hence human diet and animal husbandry had to be included. But, here again, not all of the latter, but only its fodder aspect.

To be at home in the world grain markets, one must know something about transportation—primarily freight rates, by land and sea, as well as storage, especially of course grain elevators.

Finally, to understand clearly what is going on, one needs to have an idea of what was happening before. Hence, study of the history of grain.

In the twenty years or so spent on the subject, I covered, although to a very varying degree, all these aspects. Indeed, on most of the topics, publications of mine exist (I am very disinclined to write on a subject more than once). Two books were published on the farm tractor, a pamphlet on grain elevators in the U.S.A. and Russia, and a book on the standardization of grain. A quite comprehensive issue of the Wheat Studies of the Food Research Institute, California, was devoted to the wheat of Germany. A study published in Germany in the mid 1920s dealt with production, storage, and transportation costs of grain in and from the most important exporting countries to England, the principal importing market. My study of the future of rye, made in Germany (1930), was carried as far back as statistics go, and even further, by studying a little the history of cultivated plants. It would be difficult to list everything.

Most of the accumulated knowledge, plus what had been studied specifically for the volume, was worked in in my *Competition among Grains*, a rather voluminous book, released at Stanford in January, 1940.

Since I had little formal education in anything needed for my subsequent research, I had to develop a facility for learning as I went, and at least in my case this seems to have operated with reasonable success.

After World War II, I shifted to Soviet agriculture, to land ultimately in the Soviet economy as a whole. I am not able to do everything needed even in these specialized fields, especially when it is necessary to collect all the data single-handed, which is particularly true of the last decades.

The opinion of me as a universalist has a degree of truth in it, in that I try to study the minimum of other sciences which seem necessary to handle efficiently the task in hand. This method has been pursued in all my work, including that on the economy of the U.S.S.R. At the moment of writing (late 1962) I am working on the policies followed by Khrushchev in selecting the crop pattern. The crops characteristic of Khrushchev's crop pattern are feeds (fodder, in British). I found my familiarity with the properties of the various crops as feeds wanting, and in any case not fully up to date. So I studied a little the basic contemporary works on this subject in the U.S.S.R., U.S.A., and Germany.

It seems worthwhile mentioning that such technical equipment as I have brought into my work on agricultural economics is not usual among economists. But, and I am happy to say this, it is common among the geographers. I have not met many. But those I have met were on a par with me or could beat me in familiarity with the subsidiary sciences. I am happy to say that familiarity with my *Competition among Grains* seems to be quite common among the geographers I have met. It is much greater than that among economists, for whom I intended the volume in the first place.

Naum Jasny's universalism extended well beyond the areas covered in his writings. Professor Gregory Grossman of the University of California at Berkeley tells us: "Needless to say, he lived his work and could talk endlessly about it. But it would be wrong to assume that his interests were limited to his work; on the contrary, he had the breadth of interests of a Russian intelligent, of a highly political person, and of someone who had been through a great deal and seen much."[2] Dr. J. H. Richter, in his essay in Soviet Planning, described Jasny as "a Russian embodying the best traditions of the intelligentsia of his own and earlier generations,"[3] and referred to "the stunning breadth of his knowledge and the analytical quality of his thinking."[4] Dr. Arthur Hanau, another good friend and colleague, wrote: "Naum

Jasny was a great human being and scholar of an originality that has become very rare indeed. He has made a deep impression upon me and has influenced me greatly right from the start of our acquaintance in the twenties. I owe to him a widening of my professional horizon and many other good teachings which have forever remained with me."[5]

Jasny's universalism was due in part to his extraordinarily active imagination and insatiable curiosity, which would no more allow him to ignore a hunch growing out of his research on the Soviet economy than it would permit him to remain safely aloof from the dangers of the Russian Civil War in 1918. A prodigious reader, Jasny consumed everything he could find which might touch even tangentially on a subject in which he was interested. He quickly familarized himself with every new development in the Soviet economy mentioned in the Russian press, so that in Soviet Planning Alev Nove was able to comment: "From personal experience, I have found that it is seldom possible to communicate to him a piece of information that he has not already found for himself. Thus prices and cost data on certain food products, which appeared in Moscow in January 1963 and must have reached Jasny in February or March, were already incorporated and commented upon in a fascinating manuscript which he sent for publication in March or April."[6]

Jasny's broad range of interests was reflected in the sheaves of notes and stacks of periodicals and materials for which he had to make room in his apartment. Following Jasny's retirement from the Department of Agriculture in late 1947, his apartment was taxed to the limit, having to double as his office and his living quarters. Lacking file drawers for his collection of divers materials, Jasny arranged them about the rooms of his flat, stacking them according to subject and immediacy of interest. The resulting array added to Jasny's growing reputation as an eccentric. Professor Gregory Grossman recalls the following: "On the one occasion (in the summer of 1952) that I was in his apartment I was startled to see the floor of virtually every room covered with little slips of paper bearing bits of information for his work. I assume that he knew exactly where every slip was, but it was a peculiar filing system."[7] Naum's brother Simon also was somewhat nonplused by the arrangement. One morning, after having spent the night with Naum, Simon was preparing to eat breakfast. Looking around at the tables and chairs stacked with his brother's materials, he asked, "Where can we eat?"

Naum's response was typical, "Do you have to sit down?"

Luba Richter assures us, however, that there was "a certain semblance of a system, since every subject has basically an assigned space. For a long time, material on planning was piled on the floor in front of one of his favorite chairs, and was thus adequately filed, as far as Jasny was concerned."[8]

Adding further to the confusion of papers and periodicals, about Jasny's apartment there was a colorful assortment of sea shells which Naum had gathered, washed, and put on display. Continually thinned by neighborhood children, who were urged to take their favorites home with them, the collection was replenished during Jasny's annual winter vacations in Florida.

Collecting shells, however, was only one of several hobbies which Naum Jasny enjoyed. Half hidden under a pile of papers was a television set, which enabled Jasny to pursue his favorite sports. Having enjoyed soccer when he lived in Germany, he became a baseball fan in the United States, avidly following the World Series. He was also fond of horse racing, and although he never squandered money on betting, he kept tab on the qualifications and accomplishments of the various top contenders and their jockeys. Another avocation for Jasny was bridge, which, as one might expect, appealed to his analytical mind and at which he was extraordinarily adept.

FIGHTER FOR THE TRUTH

Combining his inherent love of truth and his stubborn persistence, Naum Jasny liked to think of himself as a "fighter for the truth." In describing his early work for the Mensheviks, Jasny wrote: "I realized that organizational work, propaganda, and everything else connected with active party work just does not agree with my inclinations of an individualist and fighter for the truth, however disagreeable this may be for me."[9] This philosophy and the courage with which it was practiced have been strongly corroborated by those who knew Jasny. Dr. J. H. Richter, for example, in his essay "Naum Jasny at Eighty" wrote: "As a militant missionary endowed with great personal courage, he has pursued his mission at great personal sacrifice (for which he has an admirable capacity). He never runs from a fight and has often taken the initiative in challenging findings or points of view he believed to be wrong."[10] Professor Arthur Hanau, Jasny's friend from the twenties, referred to "his passionate quest for knowledge and his undeterrable search of truth."[11] Luba Richter, in a tribute she paid to Jasny on the occasion of his eightieth birthday, said: "His search for the truth, for facts, is coupled with a crusader's zeal in fighting for what he believes in. . . . Undoubtedly this is one of his outstanding characteristics." Gregory Grossman confirms this trait in discussing the famous Jasny-Bergson quarrel: "Behind these intellectual disputes lay Jasny's fervent concern that the Soviet economy be correctly assessed in both its weakness and its strengths. He himself was very much impressed by both—that is, the very bad performance of the Soviet economy behind the official façade of falsehoods and bravado, and the enormous potential for amassing military power that the Bolshevik totalitarian regime possessed."[12] In his introduction to Soviet Planning, Alec Nove comments: "At a relatively advanced age he plunged into detailed work about the Soviet economy because he felt deeply that serious mistakes and misunderstandings required urgent correction. . . . He regards the search for truth as a process without end, and he has never hesitated to attack those who, in his view, underestimate Soviet economic strength or who let cold war enthusiasms color their analysis or their conclusions."

This courage and commitment tended to isolate Jasny, and it probably cost him a number of friends; for no one, not even a close friend or respected colleague, was safe from attack if Jasny felt that that person was wrong. We recall, for example, the break with his great and honored compeer V. G. Groman (see above, chapter 3) over their divergent attitudes towards planning. However, although their fight, both in public and private, was vehement, the two scholars maintained their mutual respect, and years later met again as friends.

Although Jasny was thorough and devastating in his criticism, he was not always harsh. He was, in fact, usually quite gentle when correcting a friend in print. For example, when, in his Essays on the Soviet Economy, Jasny discussed Colin Clark's estimates of rate of growth, he preceded several pages of criticism with, "I am extremely sorry to have to say it, in view of the pioneering role played by Dr. Colin Clark of Oxford, England, in research on the Soviet economy (I have repeatedly emphasized my indebtedness to him in print), but . . . ."[13]

Whoever the victim, however, even when it was Jasny himself for some of his earlier errors, the "truth" as he saw it took preeminence. On this point Professor Nove wrote: "Certainly he would be the last to claim infallibility for himself. Part of his impressive output has consisted of corrections of his own ideas and figures, and the merciless criticism to which he subjects his own work should be an object lesson to all of us."[14] Acquaintances report that Jasny held especially strong convictions that acknowledging and correcting errors in print was a necessary catharsis for the analyst. In his Preface to Soviet Industrialization, 1928–1952, Jasny referred to two of his past errors, which he hoped had been corrected in the volume, and even pointed out several shortcomings in his present volume, thus anticipating some of the criticism in reviews of it. On the acknowledgment page of his monograph Essays on the Soviet Economy, he went so far as to use his motto "Through frankly acknowledged errors to the truth!"; and on page 1 he wrote:

> This writer "does not openly preach water, while secretly drinking wine" (Heinrich Heine). He actually has an irresistible urge to disassociate himself from his errors at least by frankly confessing them in print and to do this as rapidly as publishing opportunities present themselves. In 1952 the Stanford University Press published the present writer's little known statement entitled Errors and Omissions in Jasny's Monographs on the Soviet Economy, available upon request from the Press. The word 'error' was put before 'omission' advisedly. . . .
>
> Those who do not adhere to the stated principle are committing a disservice to science, to their country, and to humanity. A sort of conspiracy develops. Errors committed by others are not mentioned for the simple reason that it is hoped that one's own errors will be ignored. There is no way of knowing who still holds opinions expressed some time ago. This atmosphere is exceedingly unhealthy for the progress of research. To emphasize the vitally important principle stated, it is used as the motto of this whole book.[15]

Important virtues for Jasny were courage and persistence. To him, courage meant professing the truth, however unpopular that might be. In fact, he may have believed in an inverse ratio: the less popular the truth, the more important its dissemination. Certainly he remembered with considerable regret an occasion when he himself had not exhibited such courage, calling his failure to do so "the greatest error of my life" and confessing to "the same lack of courage of which I accuse others."[16]

In his quarrel with Abram Bergson, as in nearly every activity he undertook, Jasny displayed the stubbornness and persistence which had marked his personality since early childhood. With the tenacity of a bulldog, he grasped Bergson's tired phrase "unexampled prosperity" and shook it to death, leaving his colleagues and friends embarrassed by the corpse. The fact that Bergson had qualified his early statements with the caution that they were "not intended to constitute a blanket endorsement of 'Soviet facts'"[17] seemed to matter little to Jasny; and Jasny labeled as a "devious retreat" the fact that Bergson had gradually acknowledged that Soviet statistics were falsified.[18] Dr. George Garvy describes Jasny's tendency to overstate his case: "Jasny was quick to impute to people, with whom he did not agree, views which they didn't really hold. If somebody gave a more favorable interpretation to some Soviet statistics than Jasny did, he could easily find himself suspected of pro-Communist leanings. Jasny made a lot of enemies in the academic field."[19] Professor Grossman referred to Jasny's "persistent campaign to discredit Bergson and all those working with him," commenting: "[It] was, of course, very painful to observe by those of us who at once acknowledged Bergson's skills and achievements while holding Jasny in very high esteem as well."[20] On another occasion, Grossman wrote: "At one point, I remember clearly he assured me that his polemic against Bergson was entirely on the intellectual level and that he bore no malice against the man. I think what tended to infuriate him was that Bergson steadfastly (and to his credit) refused to cross swords with Jasny on the same polemical level."[21]

Professor Abram Bergson, who might well have wished that his opponent had been less persistent, respected Jasny's work and explains in a letter that he never really understood Jasny's hostility towards him and his colleagues:

> Jasny was obviously a distinguished scholar who contributed most significantly to our knowledge of Soviet Russia, but he was obviously also much given to polemics. I am not alone in feeling that in the case of some of the persons whose work displeased him he found it in order to go beyond the legitimate airing of scholarly differences to what can only be considered deprecatory and even defamatory personal insinuations and accusations. Such attacks, most unscholarly at any time, were only the more lamentable since they were made partly during the time of McCarthy. Unfortunately for me, I apparently was one of Jasny's favorite targets. Just why, I have never been too

clear and have been all the more puzzled since there was so much about Jasny's work that I agreed with and even admired.[22]

Jasny's attitude towards Bergson has been described by some as "paranoid."[23] Colin Clark points out that "he thought that he was being persecuted by the established authority in his field in the American universities, whom he regarded as pro-Soviet. He was very hostile to Abram Bergson, now at Harvard, though Bergson in fact reached conclusions very similar to those reached by Jasny earlier."[24] Jasny's feelings of persecution, whether wholly justified or not, were certainly very real and were understandable in view of the distorted rumors about him that apparently were circulating among the foundations in 1952 (see chapter 7) and the subsequent lack of support for the research proposals of a well established, widely recognized, and extremely productive scholar.

Although Jasny's persistence could be annoying to others, this trait proved invaluable in his research, for it made possible the infinite amount of reading necessary and the thousands of pages which he felt had to be written. Jasny's friend Hans Richter wrote, "He works with perserverance and a consuming urge";[25] and Alec Nove refers to his "tireless energy."[26] Jasny himself called it stubbornness and believed it to be an essential trait: "Stubbornness is a protective weapon in the life which fell to my lot" (see above, chapter 5). As a young man in Kharkov, when the inflating economy and alternating regimes made research virtually impossible, Jasny persevered. Likewise, as a mature analyst engaged in private research in the U.S.A., where he received "little encouragement or support,"[27] he persisted in his productive work, confident that what he had to say was important enough to justify the deprivation and frustration which he experienced.

Although Jasny's writings display the confidence which he had in the value of his research, his strong desire for recognition and approval by his peers suggests that sometimes he needed reassurance. Perhaps because of subliminal self doubts, aggravated by his lack of a doctorate, so strongly emphasized among American scholars, and the deficiency of foundation support, Jasny sought, in his colleagues' praise, a confirmation of his own capabilities. Dr. J. H. Richter wrote of his friend: "For long appropriate recognition was denied him. Without much moral or financial support, his was a bitter struggle, for he actually craved recognition both for the sake of his cause and personally." Discussing Jasny as a lecturer, Richter added: "I suspect that lecturing is precisely the thing he cherishes most among all means of professional communication. Its glamour and outward trappings of respect for the man on the rostrum have a peculiar fascination for N. J."[28] We note in his memoirs how he relished recounting the various compliments paid him and how he treasured the honors awarded him in later life. Conversely, his letters reveal the bitterness he experienced when he was not given what he felt was his due.

In his autobiography, Jasny revealed a basic modesty with statements such as "I certainly was the dumbest," "I was not a complete failure," and "with my absent-mindedness it took me some time to realize. . . ." Another example was his explanation for dedicating his Soviet Industrialization to V. G. Groman (see above, chapter 7). The present writers recall his genuine surprise upon learning in 1962 that the wife of a colleague was familiar with his Socialized Agriculture. (They also remember his indulgent twinkle as he assured her that it was not the only book he had written.) Indications of an underlying humility are found repeatedly in Jasny's writings, where he readily acknowledged the debts he owed to other scholars for research that had proved useful in his own work, and where he praised assistants, secretaries, librarians, friends, and sometimes even editors in lavish terms. Apparently fearing that he might have missed someone who deserved credit, he mentioned a number of people in his memoirs, concluding with, "I had a good assistant, Jean Hoover Ballou, during my months' work at Stanford in 1938. I would not want to leave unmentioned the several weeks in 1951 when my great friend George Denike was helping me in my work. It was a sign of the unhealthy conditions in the U.S.A. that a man of as high qualifications as Denike was compelled by financial difficulties to do auxiliary work."

PERFECTIONIST

Perfectionism is a trait frequently attributed to Jasny, especially by his editors and publishers, for nowhere was it more evident than in his constant correcting, footnoting, and rearranging of supposedly completed manuscripts.

The MS is a picture of the author. I, for example, have never in forty-seven years of writing submitted a MS without some changes, sometimes rather substantial ones, in longhand, even when the MS had already been typed more than twice. Hardly ever have I presented something for printing that has not been typed and retyped; "Competition among Grains in Classical Antiquity" was retyped more than ten times.

Even the galley proofs were not safe from his conscientious pen, and subsequent to their return, a scrawled note might well follow, requesting that the editor make one or two further, essential changes before going to press. Furthermore, every word he wrote was sacred to Jasny, for each was assigned to express the exact nuance of meaning which he wanted to convey. J. H. Richter described Jasny as a "born writer": "Often his style has elemental qualities and a feeling of discrimination for the finest shades of meanings or emphasis that rank him with the great economic authors of our time. This I believe to be true of his original writing in both English and German—neither of which is his native tongue."[29] This careful word discrimination frequently resulted in bitter arguments between Jasny and his editors, for they were committed to their own style patterns and personal connotations of words. Female editors seemed especially difficult to Jasny.

The words "Bolshevik," "Bolshevist" convey a great deal of meaning to one who has been associated with Soviet Russia for a long time. Yet one editor made quite an effort to prevent me from using those words; the party had changed its name, and this was obligatory on me in Washington, D.C., U.S.A., in her opinion. Only the proof that Khrushchev himself was using those words restrained the overzealous lady. The same editor wanted to take out the *h* in Kazakhstan, which occurred in my book perhaps twenty times. The declaration of the lady that, in the event of disagreement, her decision was final is also worth noting. Another editor deleted every zero in figures ending with it after the point, as, for example, in 27.20 rubles, not realizing that the "20" were kopeks (a ruble has 100 kopeks). On almost innumerable occasions, indeed on all of them, he replaced in the phrase "retail turnover" (as used with reference to distribution) the word "turnover" by the word "sales." There is nothing but "sales" in retail trade according to his philology. Imagine this monotony! My worst experience with editors was when one enlightened editor of a professional journal in my field asked me to remove the "bias" from my text, which dealt with the same problems (and in the same vein) as had been treated a few years earlier in my *Socialized Agriculture*, my treatment of which is now generally recognized as insufficiently critical of the Soviets on some points.

Only two American editors rated a good word from Jasny:

In the Food Research Institute nobody treated me as an ignorant ass (a later experience). The editing was good, without being excessive. Specifically, Mr. M. K. Bennet, then director of the institute and since retired, was the best editor imaginable (he was a professor of English prior to turning to economics). Professor Harry J. Carman of Columbia, who published my first book (naturally the one most affected by the defects of my English), could not have been more cordial.

European editors, however, fared better in Jasny's estimation, among them Rudolph Schlesinger, Jack Miller, and his "favorite," ironically a woman, Jane Degras.

Never forgetting the admonition of the Russian writer Nikolai Sukhanov that since he wrote about "such boring stuff," he should take his reader by the throat and shake him up, Jasny deliberately developed his style and injected his wry humor into his writings. As a result, Jasny's lively rhetoric contrasts sharply with the work of some economists who have substituted complex calculation for readable exposition and have criticized Jasny's style as "unscholarly" or "unscientific."

Ironically, one of the criticisms directed at Jasny by some fellow economists pointed to a pretermission in his research. His results sometimes were described as "informed approximations" and "rough estimates" by younger men who had been trained in the use of, and had access to, the more sophisticated tools of the trade.[30] *On this point Professor Alec Nove wrote:*

It is true that Jasny takes analytical shortcuts and makes some very rough approximations. His grasp of index numbers theory is less than perfect. . . .

His work on national income statistics and prices has been notable in several respects. He was among the first to subject the unreliable official claims to vigorous and detailed criticism. He used for this purpose methods of recalculation which were somewhat rough-and-ready and gained him some unpopularity in academic circles. Sure enough, much of what he attempted was done with much greater thoroughness by others in subsequent years. However, it took them a long time. . . . Nor have the subsequent calculations invalidated any part of Jasny's important conclusions. For example, the cost of living index and the index of prices of machinery for the period of the thirties, when they were duly calculated by highly sophisticated methods, proved very close to Jasny's rough estimates, provided early-year weights were used. Jasny is open to the criticism of never having tried a later set of weights, and there is reason to question the conceptual meaningfulness of his "real 1926/27 prices." Yet his work remains important and useful in this field also, not only as a pioneering critique but as a guide for students of Soviet statistics.[31]

Professor Grossman points to Jasny's methods as partially responsible for his quarrel with Bergson: "It was probably of little use for me to point out to him that he was not entirely correct and that much of his misapprehension stemmed from an imperfect understanding of the somewhat more sophisticated statistical techniques and economic theories than those on which his own work rested."[32]

In his defense, however, Luba Richter reminds us of Jasny's "complete lack of the most rudimentary assistance" and makes the point: "I wonder how many of us could function, year-in, year-out, without a secretary, without a typist, without a calculating machine— to say nothing of a research assistant or statistical clerk."[33] Nove, in his introduction to Soviet Planning, sums up the discussion thus:

It takes all sorts to make a world, including the academic world. The study of the Soviet economy can be approached in many different ways, and Jasny's is only one of them. Undoubtedly much has been accomplished by those using methods very different from Jasny's. There should be room in our subject for men of different methods and different temperaments. Perhaps certain arguments and methodologies now belong to an earlier period, when the area of ignorance and of dispute was much greater than it has now become. Much more is now known, not only because of the thorough work of many eminent scholars in this field, but also through much more extensive publication of statistics in the Soviet Union. Some of the short cuts

which Jasny felt compelled to take have become unnecessary. Yet we must remember the state of our knowledge
when he wrote, for instance, the three little books that were
published by Stanford University in 1951–52.[34]

Both Jasny's perfectionism and his preoccupation were reflected
in his letter writing. Well known among his friends for frequent
communications which often were little more than hastily scrawled
notes, difficult to decipher and sometimes cryptic in meaning, Jasny
was perhaps what one might call an afterthought perfectionist. The
least provocation—a scholarly inquiry, a differing opinion in print, or
merely a passing thought on Jasny's part—could elicit one of these
half- or quarter-filled pages. Frequently, however, after having mailed
the letter, Jasny had an afterthought, an addition, a clarification, a
more appropriate way of stating the point, or even an apology, which
he hastily penned and fired off on the tail of the first missive. Thus,
once a correspondence was begun, the recipient could in a short time
accumulate a sheaf of such notes. Furthermore, Jasny expected answers to his letters, thereby sometimes demanding more of his correspondent's time than the individual wished to give.

LOYAL FRIEND

Although Jasny was famous for his relentless hostility toward those
he disliked, he was nearly as well known for his intense loyalty to his
friends. The best example, perhaps, was Jasny's relationship with his
Russian friend and colleague Vladimir Gustavovich Groman, whom
Jasny admired and respected in spite of their quarrel and Groman's
eventual "confession" during the purge trials, and to whom Jasny
respectfully dedicated his Soviet Industrialization, 1928–1952. Jasny's
loyalty was especially appreciated by Dr. Otto Donner, his German
colleague of the twenties, who refers in a letter to Jasny's "warmth,
generosity, and grace as a human being." He writes:

> The clearest demonstration of these qualities I can offer
> is my own experience with him when I came to this country.
> He had, wisely, fled Germany before the war and was
> well established in his field here when I arrived in 1947.
> Here I was a German, and I had stayed in Germany and
> worked there during the war. . . . Jasny was a Jew and might
> have been expected to treat me, as did some (not all Jews)
> at best coolly. Instead, he resumed our friendship instan-

taneously, even with all its challenging discussions, human to human. I cannot tell you how much his reception, his compassion, his supportive behavior meant to me.[35]

In return for his loyalty, Jasny made relatively few, albeit significant, demands on his friends. The chief requirement was that they be willing to discuss subjects of interest to him or to listen to him expound on his latest research undertaking. His brother Simon and Simon's wife Victoria grew to expect a lecture on economics whenever Naum came to visit. J. H. Richter wrote in "Naum Jasny at Eighty": "It has sometimes been equally trying for his professional and personal friends with whom he likes to discuss endlessly the problems of interest to him—in disregard of his colleague's interests. Often, of course, there is great profit for the partner in this kind of monologue."[36] Professor Grossman writes of his relationship with Jasny:

We met at various meetings, conferences, the "unclassified forum" lunches that Leon Herman was then running in Washington for the Sovietological community, and in various government offices. Later on, we also met for lunch— just the two of us—usually in his favorite lunchroom (his *Stammlokal*, as he called it in Central European fashion) somewhere around 18th and Columbia N.W.

Needless to say, he lived his work and could talk endlessly about it . . . . Ever present in his mind was one of his early intellectual loves, the grains of antiquity. I think there was a rare meeting of ours when at some point he would not sneak in some arcane fact about Mesopotamian wheat or Roman barley.[37]

Jasny's preoccupation with his own interests, his strongly held convictions, and his compulsively blunt expression of them sometimes irritated acquaintances, but such traits were more often laughed off as minor idiosyncracies of a lovable old Russian bear.[38] Dr. Garvy, in his letter, wrote:

[Jasny] was disdainful of authority. He did not recognize any social amenities, and yet he was a man with a golden heart. He was impatient with people of mediocre talents or performance. He could be abrupt and downright unpleasant with those he didn't like. He would use harsh words to criticize minor failings.

He considered greeting people and using any conventional forms of speech as unnecessary. When I called him on the phone in Washington before taking a plane, and after a chat said that I would have to run for a plane, he just hung up.[39]

Jasny's daughters were sometimes embarrassed by their father's forthrightness. In later years Jasny frequently forgot to close his trouser fly, and when discreetly reminded by a whisper from Tanya, he would promptly zip it shut in full view of all present.

Whatever Jasny's faults, his loyalty, his warmth, and his generosity gained him a number of devoted friends and disciples, especially among those who worked for him. On this point Garvy writes: "He could be, and usually was, very considerate of people who worked for him, and I have the impression that everybody who worked for him succumbed to his charm, which I cannot define. I remember a secretary . . . who just adored him."[40]

Some have speculated that Jasny's honesty and almost childlike directness were partly responsible for his famous rapport with children. Apparently, however, there were other factors as well. His daughter Natascha tells us that Jasny was "warm and kindhearted with a great deal of love, especially for children. He never went out without some candy or lollipops in his pockets for the children in the neighborhood."[41] Dr. Richter wrote: "He loves children quite generally, particularly the smallest, and is widely known in his residential district to mothers and babies alike. For a long time there existed a regular routine for neighbourhood tots on staggered days to walk right in, go to the refrigerator, and pick one piece of candy each, with no nonsense permitted."[42] Jack Miller recalls Jasny's delight over having made friends with the children on board ship en route to Italy. Jasny's grandson Philip relates that whenever he went for a walk with his grandfather, they stopped literally at every baby carriage they encountered, so that Jasny could lean over and say something to the infant within. Jasny himself testified to his affection for children by dedicating his Soviet 1956 Statistical Handbook: A Commentary "To the little ones in general and to Linda and Phil [Tanya's children] in particular."

PATRIARCH

Nowhere was Jasny's capacity for love more evident than in his family relationships. From his memoirs we recall his patiently nursing the baby Tanya back to health and, later, his tireless devotion to Mariya as she lay dying in a hospital bed. His love was the responsible, steady, and persistent love of a patriarch, imparting warmth and security to the family about him. J. H. Richter described him as "a rock reaching out from the spiritual depths of the 19th century."[43]

During the times when money was scarce, Jasny managed one way or another to provide for his family, so that Natascha and Tanya never experienced any doubts that their needs would be met. It is true that they regarded their father as somewhat parsimonious about such things as a new dress, but whenever he saw the need was real, whether it was for food for his family, a Christmas tree for his little girls, or a college education for a grandson, Jasny willingly and generously provided the money. The annual Christmas tree, in fact, became a special symbol of Jasny's devotion to his children, for as they grew up, each year he told them they were too old for such nonsense, but every Christmas Eve he ventured out on some pretext and returned with the traditional evergreen.

Although he was occasionally firm in disciplining his children, Jasny was more often lax. Natascha remembers only one occasion when her father struck her, and that, ironically, was for being unable to solve a problem in mathematics.

Jasny especially enjoyed his role as grandfather and great-grandfather, when the responsibility was minimal and the pleasure, accordingly, greater. During the years when Tanya and her family lived around the corner from her father, Lynda and Philip enjoyed their grandfather's companionship nearly every day. They usually walked to the park across the street, where Jasny pushed them in the swings or picked them up and tossed them high into the air. Sometimes he grasped their hands tightly and swung them around and around until they all staggered with dizziness. Phil and Lynda interspersed these romps with their favorite query, confronting Jasny repeatedly with the same question, "How old are you?" His reply, to their infinite delight, was inevitably, "A hundred."

At quieter times, Lynda and Phil played in Jasny's apartment, which yielded a treasure of paper clips, rubber bands, empty fountain pens (Jasny often discarded them when they ran out of ink), and sea shells. Frequently they pursuaded "Opa" to read to them, and they listened with amusement to his heavy accent. Philip recalls wistfully that when as a small child he sucked his thumb, his grandfather often offered his own formidable appendage, urging, "Try mine."

Following the Moss's departure from Naylor Gardens, the children missed their daily frolics with their grandfather, but they did see him every Sunday, when either he came for dinner, or they went to visit him at his apartment. One Sunday at dinner, Philip recalls, Jasny decided that his grandson should know the Russian alphabet. Scribbling the letters on his greasy paper napkin, he handed it to the boy with orders to learn it. Some two hours later Jasny inquired after his grandson's progress, and was clearly disappointed that Phil had not already completed the awesome task.

As Lynda and Philip grew older and had less time for their grandfather, Jasny's great-grandchildren moved into the breach to share the "great warmth and affection" which he had for them all.

RUSSIAN

Having come to the United States at the age of fifty, Naum Jasny was never completely absorbed into the American culture. Dr. Richter, in his tribute to Jasny in Soviet Planning, refers to his friend's "deep love for his Russian motherland," going on to say:

> In many respects Jasny has failed to become integrated into the ways and psychologies of the American scene. Too much of it is alien to his unadulterated Russian nature. But despite his critical attitude toward some things in American professional life, he always pays the warmest tribute to America's great liberal traditions and to the democratic ways of its people, which he often contrasts favourably with the ways of more class-conscious societies.[44]

Like most Mensheviks during the early days of the Soviet regime, Jasny was convinced that the experiment would fail. Dr. Donner tells of his acquaintance with Jasny in Berlin:

> During our mutual days at the *Institut*, we collaborated almost exclusively in friendly arguments about the future of the USSR, in which I suppose I must confess, he took the position that it had not long to go. He supported his argument with I fear some wishful interpretations of the notorious crop failure and famine of those years and with his observations for the deprivations with which the Soviet population was paying for the intense pursuit by the Soviet regime of its policy of industrial expansion at all costs. I believe that his view owed as much to his humanity as to the political creed he held.[45]

Jasny, who was always careful to distinguish between what was Russian and what was Soviet, strongly objected to the indiscriminate substitution of the word "Russian" for the word "Soviet." In spite of his prejudice, however, Jasny's penchant for truth would not permit him to side blindly with other Menshevik émigrés. Gregory Grossman explains that during his conversations with Jasny, the latter could be "very harsh in criticizing his fellow Mensheviks when they failed to give the devil (the Soviet regime) his due, as in the case of the large underestimate of Soviet money and real wages just after the war."[46] Alec Nove reminds us that

> he has never hesitated to attack those who, in his view, underestimate Soviet economic strength or who let cold war enthusiasms colour their analysis or their conclusions. Consequently he has not been popular with anti-Soviet extremists, as witness their reaction to his ingenious attempts to calculate the number of forced labourers in the Sovet Union by using data from the 1941 plan. . . . Those who reproach him with anti-Soviet prejudices should take note of the fact that his harvest estimates for other years erred in the direction of being too high, i.e. he did not allow enough for exaggeration in the official biological yield figures.[47]

Jasny's alienation from his fellow Russians in the United States probably was an important factor in his sense of isolation in this country. It was on this note that Jasny concluded his memoirs.

It is less well known that I am not in favor with the right wing either. For many years there has been a Russian group in Georgetown University of Washington, D.C., where I have been living since 1933. The twenty years that I have been working on the Soviet economy are not enough for the group to have noticed me; or, more probably, they noticed me all right, but decided that they did not want to have anything to do with me. On the only occasion when I met people from Fordham University (the New York counterpart of Washington's Georgetown University, so far as Russian research is concerned), it was obvious that we were speaking in different languages.

So it comes that, isolated from lefts and rights, one stands rather for oneself. Specifically, in Washington, D.C., one on occasion feels almost as on a desert island. To feel really among friends, one has to cross the ocean.

Let me say in conclusion: Life is not easy for one who, not being endowed with exceptional abilities, insists nevertheless on working only on problems in which he feels he can be most successful, analyzes the problems to the limit of his capacity, and tries to publish the findings, however powerful may be those who do not like his writings. But such a life certainly is worth living. And when one is persistent enough and lives long enough, there is a good chance of achieving acceptance. To live long enough—may be the most important weapon.

Washington, D.C., 1962

Appendix

These letters are included to document Jasny's feeling that he was being discriminated against in his efforts to obtain funding for his research.

5301 Old Dominion Drive
Falls Church, Virginia
September 23, 1952

PERSONAL

Mr. Samuel Van Hyning, Jr.
Ford Foundation
1729 "H" Street, N.W.
Washington, D.C.

My dear Van Hyning:

1. For the record I briefly put down the essence of our conversation in your office on September 19. After a discussion of the form in which Mr. Jasny's project would have to be presented, you voiced concern over what one of your contacts had called "personal sniping" on the part of Mr. Jasny. Your informant, a high-ranking man in the field, had reported to you an incident that occurred in connection with the organization of a conference on East-Europe or the Soviet Union in which Mr. Jasny is said to have interfered through "personal sniping" at people connected with the conference. Mr. Jasny was also reported to have asked on one or more occasions—either in connection with the above conference or in another context—that some per-

son or persons be fired from their job. The latter report, you indicated, was second-hand.

I said that I had no knowledge of such incidents and that on general grounds, I doubted them, although it is true that Mr. Jasny did not usually mince words and never hesistated to state his opinions frankly and sometimes even bluntly.

You then proceeded to point out that, in view of the danger that there might be personal attacks in Mr. Jasny's writings under the contemplated project, you would have to ask that the sponsoring institution would assume "substantive responsibility" for the output in the sense that no such personal attacks would occur. You added that it is, of course, doubtful whether Mr. Jasny would accept such a condition. I agreed, but wanted to think it over and discuss the matter with Jasny in any case.

2. This I have now done and I must say that I am very much concerned about the situation, for a number of reasons. I am satisfied that the statements that were made to you are by no means correct; Jasny could not therefore accept the conditions that you have mentioned. If nevertheless such statements are made Jasny may be justified in believing that the group of researchers with whom he found himself in professional disagreement are trying, directly or indirectly, to eliminate him from that important field of work. This indeed would be a serious matter, especially since research on the Soviet Union is at this time of great concern to the national interest of the United States and since a monopolization of such research would therefore be a dangerous development.

3. As to Jasny's attitude regarding the conference that was mentioned to you, he was only concerned in stating the conditions under which he would participate (without having solicited the invitation that had come to him the usual way). To the Chairman of the Joint Committee of Slavic Studies of the Social Science Research Council and of the American Council of Learned Societies, under whose auspices the conference was to be held, he stated his opinion that it should not be under the chairmanship of a prominent representative of one of the groups that were at loggerheads with each other; rather that it should be chaired by someone who was not a party to the dispute. Far from suggesting himself or another representative of his views as moderator, he made the plea that the Chairman of the Joint Committee should himself assume that function. That was by no means an unreasonable suggestion; in fact, it was in accordance with customary standards of procedure in such cases. If, in presenting his proposal, Mr. Jasny hinted at the possibility of unpleasant conse-

quences for the conference if it was not accepted, he did no doubt expose his statement to misinterpretation as of querulous intent. This point, however, was immediately clarified by Jasny in writing to the Chairman of the Joint Committee so that the latter knew about its rather harmless character long before he talked to you. (I suppose it was he who gave you the conference information.)

Regarding the accusation that Jasny had asked that a person or persons be fired from their job, he assures me that this report has no foundation in fact. It is probably a variant of the other report made to you on the "conference incident."

My above statements are based on personal scrutiny of the correspondence pertaining to the controversy handed to me by Mr. Jasny. I have his permission to let you see it if you wish. I may conclude this part of my communication by saying that there are other indications of the fact that the opinions that had been reported to you are not generally shared. Thus, the Director of the Institute of World Affairs wrote me under date of September 19: "I have discussed the matter of Dr. Jasny's research with our president and we have agreed that we should be pleased to have this study carried out under the auspices of the Institute of World Affairs. . . . I will personally add that we are very happy at this possibility of having Dr. Jasny connected with us. Judging from his reputation and from his outline of his plans, we can expect him to produce an outstanding work." And to Jasny he wrote: ". . . we should consider it an honor to have your further Soviet studies carried out under our administrative auspices." The Institute has on its staff a highly qualified scholar who is fully acquainted with the international literature on the Soviet economy. It must be assumed that the opinions quoted above are voiced in that knowledge of the great impact that Jasny's work has had on our insight into the facts in this field. I may add that neither Jasny nor I have ever met the author of the above statements.

4. As to the type of controversy that has appeared in publications, I have once more scanned Mr. Jasny's writings and was unable to find that he has indulged in purely personal attacks. Naturally, where he believed to have discovered clear-cut evidence that the argument of an opponent had been invaded either by incompetence or by influences that would not serve the finding of the truth, he did voice his concern in unmistakable terms. But this any scholar would be honorbound to do—more or less drastic and colorful, depending upon temperament and courage of conviction. I have also looked at the controversy in the London "Economist" (a paper that I value as much as you do) and am really surprised that Jasny's letter (Dec. 31, 1949 issue) could possibly have given the impression you mentioned to me.

Aside from explaining three gross mistakes that the Economist's correspondent had made in his articles, Jasny drew, in measured terms, attention to the point that the correspondent's contributions had been almost entirely based (as the mistakes showed) on acceptance of Soviet statistics, many of which are nothing but propaganda. This was a perfectly legitimate warning which a journal of the Economist's high professional standard should have received with appreciation of the importance of the issues involved and with a realization of the urgency of scrutiny that this situation called for. There is not, at this time, a single analyst in this country who does not share Jasny's opinion that Soviet statistics are greatly distorted, and the only difference is that he pointed that out in 1949, while his opponents followed suit in 1952.

Mr. Jasny, in his long and distinguished career as an economist, has surely come to realize that his uncompromising attitude as a scholar and citizen has not helped smooth his path. But while personal rancour is alien to his heart, he would not compromise in the professional line. Needless to say that such criticism as appeared in Jasny's writings published by Standard University Press had been known, before publication, to his colleagues at the Food Research Institute, including the Institute's director, who invariably read his manuscripts for suggestions and discussion.

5. I have gone to this length in explaining to you the results of my inquiry for two reasons. First, because Mr. Jasny insists that the facts, as he sees them and as I see them, should be made known to you. Jasny feels strongly as you can well imagine, that he must, in the interest of a cause to which he is devoted, do whatever seems possible to clear himself of the allegations that have been made. The second reason is that, if the accusations that have been made are not correct, this would remove the basis for the condition that you have mentioned and hence the obstacle that stood in the way of the application for a grant. And this, to me, seems a very important point. For in evaluating the merits of the case we must view professional squabbles that have developed in the perspective of the extraordinary contribution to the economic research on the Soviet Union that Mr. Jasny's work has made, and continues to promise. His encyclopaedic mastery of the material and penetrating analysis have truly revolutionized the evaluation of Soviet economic developments. The issue now is whether or not the continuation of this outstanding work is to be made possible. I trust that you appreciate the import of this issue.

With kind regards,   Very sincerely yours,
                             J. H. Richter

2807 Erie St., S.E.
Washington, 20, D. C.
September 23, 1952

Dr. Merle Fainsod
Harvard University
Cambridge, 38, Mass.

Dear Dr. Fainsod: –

As you may know, the Rockefeller grant, under which I carried out research on the Soviet economy for the past four years, has come to an end. At the same time, the Food Research Institute at Stanford University and I agreed to terminate our connection since my entry upon general economic studies no longer fits the framework of the agricultural research in which the Institute is engaged.

I have made two attempts, in the recent past, to obtain the grants necessary for a continuation of my studies. Both attempts have failed—in a manner that makes me believe there are influences at work aiming to stop my research in the Soviet field. I trust that as chairman of the Joint Committee of Slavic Studies of the Social Science Research Council and the American Council of Learned Societies, you will be interested in knowing about these developments.

I would appreciate your views in this matter.

Sincerely yours,
N. JASNY

[Added by hand] I am being pushed into the extremes.
N. J.

Littauer Center M-18
Cambridge, 38, Mass.
29 September 1952

Mr. Naum Jasny
2807 Erie Street SE
Washington, 20, D. C.

Dear Mr. Jasny: –

I am sorry to hear that your Rockefeller grant has come to an end and that you have encountered difficulties in obtaining support for a continuation of your studies. While we have had differences in the past about Professor Bergson, I do believe that it is important for your researches to go on. The Joint Committee on Slavic Studies, which I chair, does not have research funds at its disposal, but if I can be of any help in facilitating an application for a research grant, I hope that you will not hesitate to call on me. If you could send me a copy of the project for which you have been trying to obtain support, I should be glad to undertake to sound out Professor Gerschenkron and other economists of my acquaintance in the hope that helpful suggestions might be forthcoming which might lead to further support of your work.

Sincerely yours,
Merle Fainsod

5301 Old Dominion Drive
Falls Church, Virginia
October 1, 1952

Mr. Samuel Van Hyning
Ford Foundation
1729 "H" Street, N.W.
Washington, D.C.

Dear Van Hyning:

Enclosed please find copy of a letter from Professor Fainsod to Mr. Jasny dated 29 September 1952 which is self-explanatory. I am glad that it supports my contention that Professor Fainsod would not see the "conference incident" in the light in which it had been reported to you.

This is in pursuance of my letter of September 23.

Sincerely yours,
J. H. Richter

Editors' Notes

CHAPTER 1—THE FAMILY AND SCHOOLING

1. February 7 under the Julian calendar, which was not adopted in Russia until 1918.
2. This point, as recalled by Simon, seems to be inconsistent with the level of wealth achieved by the elder Jasny.

CHAPTER 3—THE 1917 REVOLUTION AND THE BREAK WITH GROMAN

1. Natascha had by this time firmly established pet names for her mother and father—Mulya and Pulya. These names, plus their diminutives, are still used by both daughters in referring to their parents.
2. V. I. Lenin, "Can the Bolsheviks Retain State Power?" *Collected Works* (Moscow: Progress Publishers, 1964) 26:109-11. First published in *Prosveshcheniye*, October, 1917, no. 1-2.
3. Kharkov changed hands several times before it finally fell to the Red forces in December of 1919. Arthur E. Adams, *Bolsheviks in the Ukraine* (New Haven, Conn.: Yale University Press, 1963), p. 374.
4. A second daughter had been born in 1918.
5. Isaac Landman, ed., *The Universal Jewish Encyclopedia* (New York: Universal Jewish Encyclopedia, Inc., 1943), 10:336.
6. Adams, *Bolsheviks in the Ukraine*, p. 87.

7. David M. Lang, *A Modern History of Soviet Georgia* (New York: Grove Press, Inc., 1962), p. 235.
8. Ibid., p. 233.

CHAPTER 4—VIENNA: AN UNFULFILLED PROMISE

1. William L. Langer, ed., *An Encyclopedia of World History* (Boston: Houghton Mifflin Co., 1962), pp. 951–54, 1005–6.
2. On December 1, 1921, Vienna broke out with general disorder and plundering as workers protested in the streets at the Inner City against rising prices. See Charles A. Gulick, *Austria from Habsburg to Hitler* (2 vols.; Berkeley and Los Angeles: University of California Press, 1948), 1:129.

CHAPTER 5—GERMANY: A GOOD PLACE TO WORK

1. Yevgeniy Samoylovich Varga, born a Hungarian, served as chairman of the Hungarian Supreme Council of National Economy. Moving to Moscow in 1920, he headed the Institute for World Economy and World Politics and edited its journal. See Sergei V. Utechin, *Concise Encyclopedia of Russia* (London: J. M. Dent & Sons Ltd., 1961), p. 585.

CHAPTER 7—FREE LANCE AND BIAS

1. Luba Richter to the Lairds, March 2, 1972. Mrs. Richter was for many years the Department of State's key analyst of Soviet agriculture. More importantly for this volume, during most of Jasny's American years, she served, informally, as his research consultant, and for many of his writings of the fifties and sixties she also assisted him as editorial reader.
2. Luba Richter has told us that this research grew out of a controversy between the FEA and the OSS over the size of the Soviet grain reserves. Luba Richter to the Lairds, August 7, 1972.
3. Naum Jasny, *The Socialized Agriculture of the USSR: Plans and Performance*, p. 3.
4. Ibid., p. ix.
5. Ibid., p. viii.
6. The contract with Stanford, plus the Rockefeller grant, provided Jasny with much-needed funds until 1952, after which adequate financing posed a serious problem.

7. Alexander Baykov, *The Development of the Soviet Economic System* (Cambridge, Eng.: Cambridge University Press, 1946).

8. Jasny's contributions to *Sotsialisticheski vestnik* apparently did not begin until 1953.

9. Abram Bergson, "Appraisals of Russian Economic Statistics: A Problem in Soviet Statistics," *Review of Economic Statistics*, vol. 29, no. 4 (November, 1947), pp. 241-42.

10. Abram Bergson, "Distribution of the Earnings Bill among Industrial Workers in the Soviet Union March, 1928; October, 1934," *Journal of Political Economy*, vol. 50, no. 2 (April, 1942), p. 228.

11. Bergson to the Lairds, September 8, 1972.

12. Seymour E. Harris, "Introduction" to "Appraisals of Russian Economic Statistics," *Review of Economic Statistics*, vol. 29, no. 4 (November, 1947), p. 213.

13. Harry Schwartz and Maurice Dobb, "A Critique of 'Appraisals of Russian Economic Statistics,'" *Review of Economics and Statistics*, vol. 30, no. 1 (February, 1948), p. 38.

14. Ibid., p. 34.

15. Naum Jasny, "Soviet Statistics," *Review of Economics and Statistics*, vol. 32, no. 1 (February, 1950), pp. 92-99. Although this published version was moderate in language and polite in criticism, it is entirely possible that the original MS was less so.

16. Ibid.

17. Naum Jasny, *The Soviet Economy during the Plan Era* (Stanford University, Calif.: Stanford University Press, 1951), p. 3.

18. Naum Jasny, "Correspondence," *Soviet Studies*, vol. 8, no. 3 (January, 1957), p. 332.

19. Editor's reply to Jasny's letter in *Economist*, December 31, 1949, p. 1463. See also J. H. Richter to Van Hyning, September 23, 1952, in the Appendix to this book.

20. N. S. Timosheff, book review in *Current History*, vol. 18, no. 101, (January, 1950), p. 38.

21. Colin Clark, "Some Statistical Comparisons," in *Soviet Planning: Essays in Honour of Naum Jasny*, ed. Jane Degras and Alec Nove (Oxford, Eng.: Basil Blackwell, 1964), pp. 205-6.

22. The eight papers from that symposium were compiled in *The Soviet Union*, ed. W. Gurian (Notre Dame, Ind.: University of Notre Dame Press, 1951).

23. J. A. Kershaw, book review in *American Economic Review*, vol. 40, no. 1 (March, 1950), p. 188.

24. See "Papers and Proceedings of the Sixty-third Annual Meeting of the American Economic Association," *American Economic Review*, vol. 41, no. 2 (May, 1951), pp. 483-94.

25. Jasny, *The Soviet Economy during the Plan Era*, pp. 37-39.

26. Ibid., pp. 91-92.

27. Ibid., p. 56.

28. Ibid., p. 57.

29. Ibid., p. 65.

30. Jasny, "Correspondence," *Soviet Studies*, vol. 8, no. 3 (January, 1957), p. 332.

31. Abram Bergson, "Soviet National Income and Product in 1937: Part II: Ruble Prices and the Valuation Problem," *Quarterly Journal of Economics*, vol. 64, no. 3 (August, 1950), pp. 408-41.

32. Naum Jasny, *The Soviet Price System*, Miscellaneous Publication 11B of the Food Research Institute, Stanford University (Stanford University, Calif.: Stanford University Press, 1951), pp. 146-53.

33. Ibid., p. 153 n.101.

34. Jasny, "Correspondence," *Soviet Studies*, vol. 8, no. 3 (June, 1957), p. 333.

35. Jasny to Merle Fainsod, September 23, 1952. See Appendix.

36. J. H. Richter to Van Hyning of the Ford Foundation, September 23, 1952. See Appendix.

37. Jasny to Fainsod, September 23, 1952. See Appendix.

38. Norman Kaplan, "Arithmancy, Theomancy, and the Soviet Economy," *Journal of Political Economy*, vol. 61, no. 2 (April, 1953), pp. 110-11.

39. Jasny, "Correspondence," *Soviet Studies*, vol. 8, no. 3 (January, 1957), p. 331.

40. Naum Jasny, "On the Wrong Track," *Soviet Studies*, vol. 8, no. 1 (July, 1956), p. 72 n.1.

41. Ibid.

42. Maurice Dobb, book review in *Science and Society*, vol. 17, no. 1 (Winter, 1953), pp. 83-88.

43. Naum Jasny, "Soviet Economic Growth," *Social Research*, vol. 21, no. 1 (Spring, 1954), p. 12.

44. Ibid., p. 32.

45. Degras and Nove, *Soviet Planning*, p. 205.

46. Ibid., p. viii.

47. Hoeffding, "Correspondence," *Soviet Studies*, vol. 8, no. 2 (October, 1956), p. 215.

48. "Correspondence," *Soviet Studies*, vol. 8, no. 3 (January, 1957), p. 331.
49. Ibid.
50. At the time of his study, Jasny probably was unaware that one of those millions of inmates was his brother Vladimir, who was destined to die of a heart attack somewhere in a Siberian concentration camp. Alexander and Lev were more fortunate in that they managed to avoid arrest, and the former died in Moscow in 1951 at the age of sixty-seven. Lev, at last report, was still living in Moscow, employed part time as a chemical engineer. Apparently, he is afraid to correspond with members of his family in the U.S., and even refused to see Natascha when she visited the U.S.S.R. a few years ago.
51. Luba Richter's description of Jasny in her presentation honoring him on his eightieth birthday.
52. J. H. Richter, "Naum Jasny at Eighty," in *Soviet Planning*, p. 214.
53. Luba Richter to the Lairds, June 24, 1973.
54. Naum Jasny, preface to *Soviet Industrialization, 1928–1952* (Chicago: University of Chicago Press, 1961), pp. vii, x.
55. Ibid., p. x.
56. J. S. Prybyla, book review in *Annals of the American Academy of Political and Social Sciences*, vol. 338 (November, 1961), p. 170.
57. David Granick, book review in *American Historical Review*, vol. 67, no. 3 (April, 1962), p. 726.
58. Alexander Erlich, book review in *American Economic Review*, vol. 52, no. 4 (September, 1962), pp. 846–49.
59. After a divorce from Emil Artin, Natascha had married composer Mark Brunswick, chairman of the Music Department at the College of the City of New York.
60. Jaan Pennar to the Lairds, June 14, 1973.
61. Jack Miller to the Lairds, May 23, 1972.
62. This, as nearly as we have been able to determine, was Jasny's route, although there could be some error.
63. Naum Jasny, *Essays on the Soviet Economy*, Institute for the Study of the USSR, Munich, ser. 1, no. 63 (February, 1962), p. 6 n.4.
64. In *Soviet Agricultural and Peasant Affairs*, ed. Roy D. Laird (Lawrence: University of Kansas Press, 1963), pp. 215–47.
65. This bibliography, originally prepared by an employee at the U.S. Department of Agriculture, provided the basis for the one at the end of the present volume.

Publications by Naum Jasny

The following bibliography is based on the one that was originally included with the manuscript. Although the list has been updated and expanded, it remains incomplete, especially for the early period, many of the entries for which were from Jasny's memory. Any additions that our readers can make to the list will be greatly appreciated. —Eds.

PUBLISHED IN RUSSIAN

(Sv = Sotsialisticheskii vestnik)

Regulation of the Grain Market. Petrograd, March 8, 1917, published by the Union of Cities.

Regulation of the Food Market. Petrograd, 1917, published by the Ministry of Foods.

Can the Ukraine Be Economically Independent? Kharkov, 1918, published by Pojur.

War and the Economy. Kharkov, 1919, published by Soyuz.

"Sovremennaya Vena" (Present-day Vienna), Utro (New York), January 25, 1922.

Grain Elevators in North America and Russia. Moscow, 1925, published by Tsentrosoyuz.

Section "Grain" in the Encyclopedia of Soviet Exports, 1st ed., Berlin, 1925, 2d ed., Berlin, 1928, published by the Trade Representation of the U.S.S.R. in Germany. The second edition, written mainly by Jasny and, so far as not by him, according to his plan and edited by him, represents a small but comprehensive encylopedia of the world grain market, covering all phases of producing, marketing, processing, etc.

"Chto Rossiya budet est'?" (What will Russia eat?), Sv, no. 1 (January, 1953), pp. 3-6.

"Issledovatelskaya rabota po sovetskoi ekonomike" (Studying the Soviet economy), in The Present Situation and Future Prospects in the Political, Economic and Nationality Questions in the USSR (Proceedings of the Fourth Institute Conference in Munich-Tutzing from July 5 to 7, 1954). Vol. 1, pp. 118-24. Munich, 1954.

"S. N. Prokopovich i ischislenie narodnogo dokhoda" (S. N. Prokopovich and calculation of national income), Sv, no. 7/8 (July/August, 1955), p. 138.

"Vmesto khozyaistvennoi politiki—panatsei" (Panacea in place of economic policy), Sv, no. 10 (October, 1955), pp. 187-88.

"Voprosy rabochei sily" (Questions of the labor force), Sv, no. 4 (April, 1956), p. 72.

"Razrushenie sem'i i drugie problemy naseleniya" (Destruction of the family and other population problems), Sv, no. 7/8 (July/August, 1956), pp. 144-45.

"Industrializatsionnaya vakkhanaliya nachala 30-kh godov" (The industrialization Bacchanalia of the early 1930s), Sv, no. 12 (December, 1956), pp. 243-44.

"Medvezh'ya usluga" (Bear's help), Sv, no. 4 (April, 1957), pp. 74-75.

"Territorial'nyi razrez i tsentralizm" (Territorialization and centralism), Sv, no. 5 (May, 1957), pp. 91-93.

"Real'naya 'real'naya' zarabotnaya plata" (Real "real" wages), Sv, no. 7 (July, 1957), pp. 140-42.

"Yubileinye torzhestva i fal'shivaya statistika" (Anniversary celebrations and false statistics), Sv, no. 11 (November, 1957), pp. 215-16.

"Sel'skokhozyaistvennye itogi" (Results in agriculture), Sv, no. 2/3 (February/March, 1958), pp. 38-41.

"O realistichnosti semiletnego plana" (Reality of the Seven-Year Plan), Sv, no. 6 (June, 1959), pp. 112-13.

"Na zare planirovaniya. 1: V. G. Groman—osnovopolozhnik sovetskogo planirovaniya" (At the dawn of planning. 1: V. G. Groman—founder of Soviet planning), Sv, no. 7 (July, 1961), pp. 139-43.

"Na zare planirovaniya. 2: 1925–1929 gg." (At the dawn of planning. 2: 1925–1929), Sv, no. 8/9 (August/September, 1961), pp. 169–71.

"Na zare planirovaniya. 3: Razgrom" (At the dawn of planning. 3: Rout), Sv, no. 10/11 (October/November, 1961), pp. 199–200.

"Kul'tura neischerpaiemykh vozmozhnostei" (A crop with inexhaustible possibilities), Sv, no. 5/6(May/June, 1962), pp. 66–67.

"Khrushchev's agronomiya y fakty" (Khrushchev's agronomy and facts), Sv, no. 11/12 (November/December, 1962), pp. 171–73.

PUBLISHED IN GERMAN

(W = Wirtschaftsdienst)

"Der russische Weizen," *Landwirtschaftliche Jahrbücher*, vol. 63, no. 3 (1926), pp. 411–61.

"Der Weizenexport der Vereinigten Staaten," *Landwirtschlaftliche Jahrbücher*, vol. 66, no. 4 (1927), pp. 635–46.

"Die Weltmarktkonkurrenz von Mais und Gerste," W, vol. 13, no. 18 (May 4, 1928), pp. 818–21.

"Deutschlands Roggenausfuhr vor und nach dem Kriege," W, vol. 13, no. 25 (June 22, 1928), pp. 1018–22.

"Das Fleischproblem in den Vereinigten Staaten," W, vol. 13, no. 27 (July 6, 1928), pp. 1094–97.

"Protein und die Zukunft der Weizenproduktion," W, vol. 13, no. 30 (July 27, 1928), pp. 1219–21.

"Die Getreideterminbörse in Chicago," W, vol. 13, no. 33 (August 17, 1928), pp. 1333–36.

"Der Mähdrescher in der überseeischen Landwirtschaft," W, vol. 13, no. 36 (September 7, 1928), pp. 1456–58.

"Die Lage des Weltmarktes für Brotgetreide," W, vol. 13, no. 38 (September 21, 1928), pp. 1544–47.

"Die Lage des Weltmarktes für Futtergetreide," W, vol. 13, no. 40 (October 5, 1928), pp. 1628–31.

"Die Aufgaben des Internationalen Landwirtschaftlichen Instituts in Rom," W, vol. 13, no. 44 (November 2, 1928), pp. 1797–99.

"Die Traktoren in der überseeischen Landwirtschaft," W, vol. 13, no. 47 (November 23, 1928), pp. 1930–32.

"Stabilisierung der Getreidepreise," W, vol. 13, no. 49 (December 7, 1928), pp. 2009–12.

"Entwicklung des überseeischen Getreideanbaus," W, Part 1: vol. 13, no. 51 (December 21, 1928), pp. 2103–7; Part 2: vol. 13, no. 52 (December 28, 1928), pp. 2150–54.

"Die Getreide-, Mehl- und Futtermittelhandlung," *Wirtschafts-Jahrbuch*, 1928, pp. 202–7.

"Die Konkurrenzfähigkeit der wichtigsten Überseeländer auf dem Weizenweltmarkt," *Berichte über Landwirtschaft*, N.F., vol. 9, no. 1/2 (1929), pp. 1–68.

"Die deutsche Getreideernte," W, vol. 14, no. 3 (January 18, 1929), pp. 91–94.

"Der Kanadische Getreidepool," W, vol. 14, no. 6 (February 8, 1929), pp. 210–14.

"Die Lage der Getreidemärkte," W, vol. 14, no. 8 (February 22, 1929), pp. 338–39.

"Di Zukunft der Sojabohne," W, vol. 14, no. 9 (March 1, 1929), pp. 353–56.

"Zum Plan einer Marktausgleichsgebühr für Weizen," W, vol. 14, no. 11 (March 15, 1929), pp. 441–43.

"Schweizer: Ende des Getreidemonopols," W, vol. 14, no. 12 (March 22, 1929), pp. 508–10.

"Der Weltweizenmarkt," W, Part 1: "Produktion und Verbrauch," vol. 14, no. 16 (April 19, 1929), pp. 673–75; Part 2: "Einfuhr und Ausfuhr," vol. 14, no. 17 (April 26, 1929), pp. 719–23.

"Farmerhilfe in den Vereinigten Staaten von Nord-Amerika," W, vol. 14, no. 20 (May 17, 1929), pp. 841–44.

"Die Baisse auf den Getreidemärkten," W, vol. 14, no. 23 (June 7, 1929), pp. 966–69.

"Neuordnung der Getreidewirtschaft," W, vol. 14, no. 27 (July 5, 1929), pp. 1141–45.

"Die Weltmärkte für Weizenmehl," W, vol. 14, no. 31 (August 2, 1929), pp. 1323–28.

"Die Getreideweltmärkte im Jahre 1928/29," W, vol. 14, no. 33 (August 16, 1929), pp. 1410–13.

"Das Erntejahr '28/'29 in Deutschland," W, vol. 14, no. 36 (September 6, 1929), pp. 1536–39.

"Die Neuordnung der deutschen Getreidewirtschaft," W, vol. 15, no. 2 (January 10, 1930), pp. 44–46.

"Die Weltgetreidemärkte," W, vol. 15, no. 39 (September 26, 1930), pp. 1657–60.

"Die deutschen Brotgetreidemärkte," W, vol. 15, no. 41 (October 10, 1930), pp. 1741–44.

"Die 'Wheat Studies' des kalifornischen Food Research Institute," *Archiv, weltwirtschaftliches*, vol. 30 (1930), pp. 129–41.

Die neuzeitliche Umstellung der überseeischen Getreideproduktion und ihr Einfluss auf Weltmarkt. Sonderheft 16 der Vierteljahrshefte zur Konjunkturforschung, Institut für Konjunktur-forschung. Berlin: R. Hobbing, 1930. 88 pp.

Die Zukunft des Roggens. Sonderheft 20 der Vierteljahrshefte zur Konjunkturforschung, Institut für Konjunkturforschung. Berlin: R. Hobbing, 1930.

(Together with A. Hanau) "Die Märkte der Wichtigsten landwirt-schaftlichen Produkte," in Handbuch der Landwirtschaft, edited by Aereboe, Hansen, and Roemer. Berlin: P. Parey, 1930.

Bevölkerungsgang und Landwirtschaft Wirkung des verlangsamten Bevölkergszunahme auf Konsumgestaltung. Schriftenreihe des Institut für landwirtschaftliche Marktforschung, no. 2. Berlin: P. Parey, 1931. 88 pp.

"Bevölkerungswachstum und Landwirtschaft," Blätter für landwirt-schaftliche Marktforschung, vol. 1, no. 9 (February, 1931), pp. 335–42.

"Struktur der deutschen Mühlenindustrie," Blätter für landwirtschaft-liche Marktforschung, vol. 1, no. 10 (March, 1931), pp. 461–73.

"Deutsche Roggenpolitik," Deutscher Volkswirt, no. 28 (April 10, 1931); no. 29 (April 17, 1931); no. 30 (April 24, 1931).

"Die Weltagrarkrise," Blätter für landwirtschaftliche Marktforschung, vol. 1, no. 12 (May, 1931), pp. 571–86.

Der Schlepper in der Landwirtschaft, seine Wirtschaftlichkeit und weltwirtschaftliche Bedeutung. Berlin: P. Parey, 1932. 155 pp. (Reichsministerium für Ernährung und Landwirtschaft. Berichte über Landwirtschaft, N.F. Sonderheft 62.)

Die Standardisierung von Getreide. Schriftenreihe des Institut für landwirtschaftliche Marktforschung, no. 4. Berlin, 1932. 151 pp.

"Die Lage am Getreidemarkt," Blätter für landwirtschaftliche Markt-forschung, vol. 3, no. 6 (November, 1932) pp. 233–51.

(Together with A. Hanau) "Die deutsche Getreidebilanz," Blätter für landwirtschaftliche Marktforschung, vol. 3 (1933), pp. 131–49 and 307–17.

"Zum Weltgetreideproblem," Blätter für landwirtschaftliche Markt-forschung, vol. 3 (1933), pp. 510–17.

Review of Carl Boehm's Die Elastizitat der deutschen Getreide-Anbauflachen, Reviews, vol. 19, no. 4 (November, 1937), pp. 959–60.

"Soviet Planning." In Beiträge zur empirischen Konjunkturforschung. Festschrift zum 25th jährigen Bestehen des Deutschen Instituts für Wirtschaftsforschung. Berlin, 1950. Pp. 179–207.

"International Organisationen und Sowjetstatistik," Ost-Probleme, vol. 2 (1950), pp. 1086–92.

"Probleme der Grosskolchose," *Ost-Probleme*, vol. 3 (1951), pp. 1280–82.

"Sklavenarbeit und Produktion," *Ost-Probleme*, vol. 3 (1951), pp. 1553–62.

"Die Landwirtschaft im 5. sowjetischen Fünfjahresplan," *Agrarwirtschaft*, vol. 2 (February, 1953), pp. 60–65.

"Der neue Kurs in der sowjetischen Landwirtschaft," *Agrarwirtschaft*, vol. 3 (February, 1954), pp. 40–45.

"Der sowjetische Staatshaushalt," *Finanzarchiv*, vol. 15, no. 1 (1954), pp. 125–70; vol. 15, no. 3 (1955), pp. 530–35.

"Der sowjetische Staatshaushalt 1956," *Osteuropa-Wirtschaft*, vol. 1, no. 1 (August, 1956), pp. 33–40.

"Die Zuwachsraten der sowjetischen Wirtschaft," *Konjunkturpolitik*, no. 2 (1956), pp. 74–84.

"Chruschtschow und die Sowjetwirtschaft," *Ost Europa*, vol. 7, no. 10 (October, 1957), pp. 709–18.

"Die Landwirtschaft in der Sowjetunion," *Agrarwirtschaft*, vol. 7, no. 8 (August, 1958), pp. 248–55.

"Vergleich der Kolchosbauern- und Arbeitereinkommen in der Sowjetunion: ein vernachlässigtes Thema," *Berichte über Landwirtschaft*, N.F., vol. 39 (1969). (An updating of the English article.)

PUBLISHED IN FRENCH

"L'agriculture soviétique," *Le Contrat Social*, vol. 2, no. 3 (May, 1958), pp. 152–58. (Translated from English.)

"De l'interprétation des statistiques soviétiques," *Le Contrat Social*, vol. 3, no. 1 (January, 1959), pp. 45–48. (Translated from English.)

"Revenus des paysons et des ouvriers en U.R.S.S.," *Le Contrat Social*, vol. 4, no. 5 (September, 1960), pp. 303–7. (Translated from English.)

"Étapes du développement économique en U.R.S.S.," *Le Contrat Social*, vol. 5, no. 4 (July/August, 1961), pp. 215–22. (Translated extracts from *Soviet Industrialization, 1928–1952*.)

"L'agriculture soviétique dix ans après Staline," *Le Contrat Social*, vol. 8, no. 4 (July/August, 1964), pp. 214–20. (Translated from Russian.)

PUBLISHED IN ENGLISH: AGRICULTURAL ECONOMICS (OTHER THAN U.S.S.R.)

"Tractor versus Horse as a Source of Farm Power," *American Economic Review*, vol. 25, no. 4 (December, 1935), pp. 708–23.

"Wheat Problems and Policies in Germany." In *Wheat Studies* (Stanford University, Calif.: Food Research Institute, 1936), vol. 13, no. 3, pp. 65–140.

Research Methods on Farm Use of Tractors. Columbia University Studies in the History of American Agriculture, edited by Harry J. Carman and Rexford G. Tugwell, vol. 5. New York: Columbia University Press, 1938. 273 pp.

Competition among Grains. Grain Economic Series of Stanford University, Food Research Institute. Vol. 2. Stanford University, Calif., 1940. 606 pp.

"Proposal for Revision of *Agricultural Statistics*," *Journal of Farm Economics*, vol. 24, no. 2 (May, 1942), pp. 402–19.

Price and Cost of Bread in the United States and Other Countries. U.S.D.A., Bureau of Agricultural Economics, Washington, D.C., June, 1943. (For administrative use only.)

"Decline and Recovery in European Agriculture: World Wars I and II," *Foreign Agriculture*, vol. 10 (April/May, 1946), pp. 66–75.

Recovery in European Agriculture, World Wars I and II, U.S.D.A., Office of Foreign Agriculture, 1946. 14 pp.

Agricultural Geography of Europe and the Near East. (Atlas) U.S.D.A. Misc. Pub. 665, 1948. 67 pp. By L. B. Bacon and others. N. Jasny, associate author.

"Germany's Capacity to Produce Agricultural Products," *Foreign Agriculture*, vol. 21, no. 5 (May, 1957), pp. 217–56.

PUBLISHED IN ENGLISH: CLASSICAL ANTIQUITY (GRAIN, FLOUR, BREAD)

"Competition among Grains in Classical Antiquity," *American Historical Review*, vol. 47, no. 4 (July, 1942), pp. 747–64.

"Wheat Prices and Milling Costs in Classical Rome." In *Wheat Studies* (Stanford University, Calif.: Food Research Institute, 1944), vol. 20, no. 4, pp. 137–70.

The Wheats of Classical Antiquity. The Johns Hopkins University Studies in Historical and Political Science, ser. 62, no. 3. Baltimore, Md.: The Johns Hopkins Press, 1944. 176 pp.

"The Breads of Ephesus and Their Prices," *Agricultural History,* vol. 21, no. 1 (July, 1947), pp. 190–92.

"The Daily Bread of the Ancient Greeks and Romans," *Osiris* 9 (1950):227–53.

PUBLISHED IN ENGLISH: AGRICULTURE OF U.S.S.R.

"Labor Productivity in Agriculture in USSR and USA," *Journal of Farm Economics*, vol. 27, no. 2 (May, 1945), pp. 419–32.

"Unirrigated Cotton in Southern Russia and the Danubian Countries," *Foreign Agriculture*, vol. 11, no. 1 (January, 1947), pp. 2–14.

"The Plight of the Collective Farms," *Journal of Farm Economics*, vol. 30, no. 2 (May, 1948), pp. 304–21.

"Soviet Agriculture and the Fourth Five-Year Plan," *Russian Review*, vol. 8, no. 2 (April, 1949), pp. 135–41.

"USSR: Law on Measures to Ensure High and Stable Yields in the Steppe and Forest-Steppe Regions," *Land Economics*, vol. 25, no. 4 (November, 1949), pp. 351–58.

The Socialized Agriculture of the USSR: Plans and Performance. Stanford, Calif.: Stanford University Press, 1949. 837 pp.

"Kolkhozy, the Achilles' Heel of the Soviet Regime," *Soviet Studies*, vol. 3, no. 2 (October, 1951), pp. 150–63.

"Soviet Grain Crops and Their Distribution," *International Affairs*, vol. 28, no. 4 (October, 1952), pp. 452–59.

"Prospects for Soviet Farm Output and Labor," *Review of Economics and Statistics*, vol. 36, no. 2 (May, 1954), pp. 212–19.

"More Soviet Grain Statistics," *International Affairs*, vol. 32, no. 4 (October, 1956), pp. 464–66.

"Russia's Big Weakness: There's Not Enough to Eat," *U.S. News and World Report*, September 13, 1957, pp. 70–77.

"Soviet Agriculture," *Current History*, vol. 34, no. 197 (January, 1958), pp. 21–27. (Translated into French.)

"Low- and High-Yielding Crops in the USSR." In *Soviet Agricultural and Peasant Affairs*, edited by Roy D. Laird. Lawrence: University of Kansas Press, 1963. Pp. 215–47.

"The Failure of the Soviet Animal Industry," *Soviet Studies*, Part 1: vol. 15, no. 2 (October, 1963), pp. 187–218; and Part 2: vol. 15, no. 3 (January, 1964), pp. 285–307.

Khrushchev's Crop Policy. Glasgow, Scotland: George Outram, for Insitute of Soviet and East European Studies, University of Glasgow, [1965]. 243 pp.

"Production Costs and Prices in Soviet Agriculture." In *Soviet and East European Agriculture*, edited by Jerzy F. Karcz. Berkeley and Los Angeles: University of California Press, 1967. Pp. 212–57.

PUBLISHED IN ENGLISH: ECONOMY OF THE U.S.S.R.
OTHER THAN AGRICULTURE

"Intricacies of Russian National-Income Indexes," *Journal of Political Economy*, vol. 55, no. 4 (August, 1947), pp. 299–322.

"Soviet Statistics," *Review of Economics and Statistics*, vol. 32, no. 1 (February, 1950), pp. 92–99.

"International Organizations and Soviet Statistics," *Journal of the American Statistical Association*, vol. 45, no. 249 (March, 1950), pp. 48–64. (Translated into German.)

"The Soviet Price System," *American Economic Review*, vol. 40, no. 5 (December, 1950), pp. 845–63.

Discussion of Papers: "Soviet Agricultural Collectivism in Peace and War," by Lazar Volin, and "The Economic War Potential of the U.S.S.R.," by Joseph A. Kershaw, *American Economic Review*, vol. 41, no. 2 (May, 1951), pp. 484–94. Papers and Proceedings of the Sixty-third Annual Meeting of the American Economic Association, Chicago, Illinois, December 27–30, 1950.

"Labor and Output in Soviet Concentration Camps," *Journal of Political Economy*, vol. 59, no. 5 (October, 1951), pp. 405–19.

"Results of Soviet Five-Year Plans." In *The Soviet Union*, edited by Waldemar Gurian. Notre Dame, Ind.: University of Notre Dame Press, 1951. Pp. 30–63.

The Soviet Economy during the Plan Era. Food Research Institute, Stanford University, Miscellaneous Publication 11A. Stanford University, Calif.: Stanford University Press, 1951. 116 pp.

The Soviet Price System. Food Research Institute, Stanford University, Miscellaneous Publication 11B. Stanford University, Calif.: Stanford University Press, 1951. 179 pp.

"A Close-up of the Soviet Fourth Five-Year Plan," *Quarterly Journal of Economics*, vol. 66, no. 2 (May, 1952), pp. 139–71.

Soviet Prices of Producers' Goods. Food Research Institute, Stanford University, Miscellaneous Publication 11C. Stanford University, Calif.: Stanford University Press, 1952. 180 pp.

Errors and Omissions in Jasny's Monographs on the Soviet Union. Stanford, Calif.: Stanford University Press, 1952. 2 pp.

"The New Economic Course in the USSR," *Problems of Communism*, vol. 3, no. 1 (January/February, 1954), pp. 8–14. (Reprinted from *Twentieth Century*, London, November, 1953.)

"A Soviet Planner—V. G. Groman," *Russian Review*, vol. 13, no. 1 (January, 1954), pp. 52–58.

"Soviet Economic Growth," *Social Research*, vol. 21, no. 1 (Spring, 1954), pp. 11–42.

"Price of Soviet 'Progress': Real Wages below 1928 Level," *Daily Telegraph & Morning Post* (London), May 31, 1954.

"Some Problems in Soviet Statistics," *American Statistician*, vol. 9, no. 2 (April, 1955), pp. 22–24.

Indices of Soviet Industrial Production, 1928–54. Corporation for
Economic and Industry Research, Report A-46. Washington,
D.C., 1955.

"On the Wrong Track," *Soviet Studies*, vol. 8, no. 1 (July, 1956),
pp. 50–76.

"The Soviet Population of 1956," *American Statistician*, vol. 11, no. 1
(February, 1957), pp. 18–20.

"Death Rates and Living Standards in the Soviet Union," *American
Statistician*, vol. 11, no. 4 (October, 1957), pp. 18–20.

The Soviet 1956 Statistical Handbook: A Commentary. East Lan-
sing: Michigan State University Press, 1957. 212 pp.

"The Rates of Soviet Economic Growth," *American Statistician*, vol.
12, no. 3 (June, 1958), pp. 21–24.

"Penny Plain, Twopence Coloured: Interpreting Soviet Statistics,"
Soviet Survey, no. 26 (October–December, 1958), pp. 9–14. Re-
produced in three symposiums in the U.S.A. and also by the War
Academy in Washington, D.C. (Translated into French.)

"Some Thoughts on Soviet Statistics: An Evaluation," *International
Affairs*, vol. 35, no. 1 (January, 1959), pp. 53–60.

" 'A Mighty Maze! But Not without a Plan': Soviet Economy:
Target for Tomorrow," *Soviet Survey*, no. 27 (January–March,
1959), pp. 57–62.

"The Soviet Seven-Year Plan: Is It Realistic?" *Bulletin of the Institute for the Study of the USSR*, vol. 6, no. 5 (May, 1959), pp.
21–28.

"Peasant-Worker Income Relationships: A Neglected Subject," *Soviet Studies*, vol. 12, no. 1 (July, 1960), pp. 14–22. (Translated
into French and German.)

"On Professor Polanyi's Thesis," *Soviet Survey*, no. 34 (October–
December, 1960), pp. 103–4. (Comments on Michael Polanyi's
"Towards a Theory of Conspicuous Production," pp. 90–99.)

"A Note on Rationality and Efficiency in the Soviet Economy," *Soviet Studies*, Part 1: vol. 12, no. 4 (April, 1961), pp. 353–75;
Part 2: vol. 13, no. 1 (July, 1961), pp. 35–68.

"Stages of Soviet Economic Development," *Survey*, no. 37 (July–
September, 1961), pp. 24–33. (Translated into French.)

"Improving Soviet Planning: Thirty-Five Years of Mediocrity,"
International Affairs, vol. 37, no. 4 (October, 1961), pp. 465–76.
(Translated into French.)

"The Price of Soviet Industrialization," *Current History*, vol. 41, no.
243 (November, 1961), pp. 292–98.

"Plan and Superplan," *Survey*, no. 38 (October, 1961), pp. 29–43.

Soviet Industrialization, 1928–1952. Chicago: University of Chicago Press, 1961. 467 pp.

"Rationality and Efficiency: A Further Note," *Soviet Studies,* vol. 13, no. 3 (January, 1962), pp. 321–23.

"How 'Phoney' Are Soviet Statistics?" *Statist,* vol. 175, no. 4378 (February 2, 1962), pp. 329–30.

"Soviet Statistical Yearbooks for 1955 through 1960," *Slavic Review,* vol. 21, no. 1 (March, 1962), pp. 121–56.

"The Secret 1941 Uzbek Economic Plan," *Soviet Studies,* vol. 13, no. 4 (April, 1962), pp. 407–13.

"The Russian Economic 'Balance' and Input-Output Analysis: A Historical Comment," *Soviet Studies,* vol. 14, no. 1 (July, 1962), pp. 75–80. (Translated into French.) (Also published as "The Soviet Balance of National Income and the American Input-Output Analysis," Editrice *L'industria, Milano,* no. 1 [Milan, 1962], pp. 3–9.)

Essays on the Soviet Economy. New York: Praeger, 1962; and Munich: Institute for the Study of the USSR, 1962. 297 pp.

"Prospects of the Soviet Iron and Steel Industry," *Soviet Studies,* vol. 14, no. 3 (January, 1963), pp. 275–94.

"A Short Cut to Growth Rates in Soviet National Income," *Soviet Studies,* vol. 15, no. 1 (July, 1963), pp. 38–42.

Review of Boris Nikolaevsky's *Power and the Soviet Elite,* in *Soviet Studies,* vol. 18, no. 1 (July, 1966), pp. 105–7.

Soviet Economists of the Twenties: Names to Be Remembered. Vol. 1 of Soviet and East European Studies. Cambridge, Eng.: At the University Press, 1972. 218 pp.

Index

Cherevanin, Fedor A., 20, 24, 31
Chkheidze, Nikolai S., 29
Chuprov, Alexander, 9
Chuprov Society, 17
Cities, Union of, 14–16, 19, 22, 33, 34
Clark, Colin, 113, 114, 116, 124, 132, 148, 151
Clark, Gardner, 127–28, 132
Competition among Grains, 83–84, 144, 145

Degras, Jane, 81, 136, 138, 154
Demosfenov, 18
Den, 32; articles in, 34
Denike, George, 134, 137, 152
Denikin, Anton I., 39, 42
Devdariani, Seid, 43
Dobb, Maurice, 113–14, 119, 123
Dolinski, 18
Donner, Otto, 66, 70, 156–57, 160

Economist, The, 115
Erlich, Alexander, 133
Essays on the Soviet Economy, 136, 142, 148, 149

FEA (Foreign Economic Administration), 72 n, 108–9
Flour Bureau, Central, 22, 24, 31
Flyaksberger, 63
Food, Ministry of, 35, 36 n, 42
Food, Special Council for, 19, 22, 23, 24
Food Board, All-State, 34
Food Commission, 29–30, 31, 36
Food Council, Central, 21
Food Research Institute, 83, 109, 118, 121, 144, 154
Frankel, Hans, 132

Garvy, George (Jura), 66, 70, 72, 150, 157, 158
Garvy, Peter, 11
Georgia, 42–45, 50
Gerschenkron, Alexander, 113, 114
Grannick, David, 133
Graser, Elsa Rose, 94
Greenslade, Russell, 137

Groman, Vladimir G., 15–34, 36, 60, 133, 148, 152, 156
Grossman, Gregory, 145, 146, 148, 150, 155, 157, 161

Hamburg, 61–63, 64, 83
Hanau, Arthur, 65, 70, 124, 135, 145, 147–48
Harris, Seymour E., 113
Herman, Leon, 157
Hoeffding, Oleg, 125

Imperial Free Economic Society, 24, 43
Institute for the Study of the U.S.S.R., 124–25, 134–38 passim
Institut für Konjunkturforschung (IFK), 62, 65–70, 72
Institut für Landwirtschaftliche Marktforschung, 69 n, 70–75

Jakobson, Roman, 13
Jasny, Alexander (brother), 3, 5, 7, 26
Jasny, Lev (brother), 3, 5, 7, 26, 27–28
Jasny, Michael (father), 3–5, 9, 12, 26, 38, 53, 59–60, 79, 82, 84, 107
Jasny, Natalie ("Natascha") (daughter) (Mrs. Emil Artin, now Mrs. Mark Brunswick), 14, 26–28, 40, 41, 44–45, 49, 50, 57–58, 59, 60, 64, 73, 83, 134, 135, 136, 158, 159
Jasny, Mrs. Naum (Maria Phillipi Jasny) ("Philya"), 74, 75, 79, 80, 83, 84, 135
Jasny, Mrs. Naum (Mariya Orlova Jasny) ("Mulya"), 13–14, 26–27, 39, 40–42, 44–45, 50, 62, 64, 73, 74, 159
Jasny, Rosa (mother), 3–5, 7, 12–13, 38, 53, 79, 82
Jasny, Simon (brother), 3, 5, 7, 12, 26, 27, 38, 58, 79, 84, 107, 146–47, 157
Jasny, Sonya (sister), 3, 5, 7
Jasny, Tatyana ("Tanya") (daughter) (Mrs. Milton Moss), 41–42, 44–45, 49, 50, 59, 60, 64, 73, 74, 75, 80,